EXERCISE BOOKLET

to accompany

ALONG THESE LINES
WRITING PARAGRAPHS AND ESSAYS

THIRD CANADIAN EDITION

John Sheridan Biays
Broward Community College

Carol Wershoven
Palm Beach Community College

Lara Sauer
George Brown College

Pearson Canada
Toronto

This edition for sale only in Canada

ISBN-13: 978-0-13-207151-2
ISBN-10: 0-13-207151-7

Acquisitions Editor: David LeGallais
Senior Developmental Editor: Patti Altridge
Marketing Manager: Loula March
Production Coordinator: Janis Raisen
Production Editor: Claire Horsnell

3 4 5 DPC 11 10 09

Printed and bound in Canada

Table of Contents

Exercises for Writing in Steps: The Process Approach

CHAPTER 1: WRITING A PARAGRAPH

Creating Questions for Brainstorming

Below are several topics. For each one, brainstorm by writing at least six related questions that could lead to further detail. The first topic is done for you.

a. topic: bills

Question 1: *Why do I hate bills?*

Question 2: *Is it because I never have enough money?*

Question 3: *Or is it because I'd rather spend the money on something else?*

Question 4: *How many bills do I get every month?*

Question 5: *What kinds of bills are they?*

Question 6: *What bills are the ones I hate most?*

b. topic: computers

Question 1: _____

Question 2: _____

Question 3: _____

Question 4: _____

Question 5: _____

Question 6: _____

c. topic: jobs

Question 1: _____

Question 2: _____

Question 3: _____

Question 4: _____

Question 5: _____

Question 6: _____

d.　　topic: crime

Question 1: _____

Question 2: _____

Question 3: _____

Question 4: _____

Question 5: _____

Question 6: _____

e.　　topic: debt

Question 1: _____

Question 2: _____

Question 3: _____

Question 4: _____

Question 5: _____

Question 6: _____

CHAPTER 1: WRITING A PARAGRAPH

Finding Specific Details in Freewriting

You can do this exercise on your own, with a partner, or with a group. Below are two samples of freewriting. Each is a written response to a different topic. Read each sample, and then underline any words and phrases that could become the focus of a paragraph.

Freewriting on the Topic of Doing Errands

Don't mind doing errands if I have enough time. Never seem to have enough time, however. Always seem to be racing around. Picking up dry cleaning. Going to bank. Shopping at supermarket. The supermarket is the easiest errand because I like to buy goodies. Never buy food when you're hungry, experts say. I try to do errands at lunch hour. Then I get frustrated by lack of time.

Freewriting on the Topic of Vacations

Family vacations. When I was a kid, we went to the beach every summer. Water was so cold! Always took a plastic raft. Dad had to blow it up. Now, kids take those long noodle things, water wings, snorkel masks, fins. Lots of new water toys. Times change. Different attitudes towards the sun at beach too. Used to be baby oil and basking in the sun for hours. Now, slather on the sunblock and sit under an umbrella..

CHAPTER 1: WRITING A PARAGRAPH

Writing Topic Sentences for Lists of Details

Below are lists of details that have no point, no topic sentence. Write an appropriate topic sentence for each one.

a.   topic sentence: ————————————————————

————————————————————

Contact with nature helps relieve stress.
Plants and trees renew our sense of wonder.
A few minutes outdoors reconnects us to the rhythm of the seasons.
Meditating in a garden can bring peace.
The sound of running water is said to be calming.

b.   topic sentence: ————————————————————

————————————————————

I'm used to texting, instant messaging, and e-mailing
I use my laptop to take notes in class.
My handwriting is sloppy and writing makes my hand cramp.
Carrying my laptop, textbooks and other items makes my shoulder sore.
Some days my bag must weigh more than 25 pounds.
I frequently can't access the wireless network on campus.

c.   topic sentence: ————————————————————

————————————————————

Amy and Roberto married for love.
Celestine and Francoise married out of loneliness.
Annelle's parents pressured Annelle and Jim to get married.
Bob and Selena married on the rebound.
Tim married Christine for financial security.

CHAPTER 1: WRITING A PARAGRAPH

Adding Details to Support a Topic Sentence

The topic sentences below have some—but not enough—details. Write sentences to add details to the list below each topic sentence.

a.   topic sentence: In the past year, I have bought several items I don't need.

    1. I spent a fortune on a plasma TV.
    2. When I brought it home, I realized it didn't fit in my living room.

    3. _____

    4. _____

    5. _____

    6. _____

b.   topic sentence: Waiting at the doctor's office is very stressful.

    1. The doctor is always running late.
    2. Sometimes I wait for an hour.
    3. The waiting room is always crowded.

    4. _____

    5. _____

    6. _____

c.   topic sentence: I know several quiet places where I can relax.

    1. I love to walk in the woods.
    2. The stillness and the cool green setting soothe me.

    3. _____

    4. _____

    5. _____

    6. _____

CHAPTER 1: WRITING A PARAGRAPH

Revising a Rough Lines Draft by Combining Sentences

The paragraph below has many short, choppy sentences. The short, choppy sentences are underlined. Wherever you see two or more underlined sentences clustered next to each other, combine the clustered sentences into one, clear, smooth sentence. Write your revised version of the paragraph in the spaces above the lines.

My little sister has too many toys. Megan has six huge stuffed animals. They cover her bed. She has a variety of dolls. My aunt gave her Hanna Montana. My cousin gave her two dolls that look like characters from *High School Musical*. My mother bought her a Cinderella doll. If she gets tired of dolls, Megan has other toys. She has a toy kitchen with a plastic table, stove, and refrigerator. She has an elegant doll's house, too. Megan has toys for every occasion and location. She owns beach toys. She has bath toys. She also has toys for the car and toys for bedtime. She has so many toys, she has nowhere to put them. They are scattered all over the house. I can't help tripping over them.

CHAPTER 1: WRITING A PARAGRAPH

Correcting Errors in Final Lines

Proofread the paragraph below, looking for errors in spelling, punctuation, mechanics, and word choice. Correct the errors by crossing out each mistake and writing the correction above it.

      Some people think that all Italian food is bad for you, but they are mistaken. For one thing, studies have prove that olive oil, which is a common ingredient in Italian food, can be good for you. It can have a healthy affect on cholestrol levels. And while many people think Italian food is fattening, it don't have to be. There are many things on an Italian menu, like fresh fruit's and vegetable's, chicken, and fish. Many people think all pasta is fattening, but pasta doesn't have to be fattening its what you put on it that counts. A delicious sauce made from fresh tomatoes, garlic, and herbs can be healthy and low in calories. Italian cooking has so much variety, it has something for every kind of eater from the health-conscience to the dietor.

CHAPTER 2: WRITING FROM READING

Paraphrasing

Paraphrase the following paragraph, taken from the Citizenship and Immigration Canada website:

In 2006, approximately 260,000 people became Canadian citizens and took an oath of citizenship at ceremonies across the country. The oath is a personal commitment to accept the responsibilities and privileges of Canadian citizenship[1].

_____

_____

_____

_____

Correcting the Errors in a Final Lines Reaction to a Reading

Proofread the paragraph below, looking for errors in spelling, punctuation, mechanics, sentence structure, and word choice. Correct the errors by crossing out each mistake and writing the correction above it.

Looking for a close parking spot is silly, Gwinn Owens says,and I agree with him. My mother spend twenty minutes driving around a parking lot, looking for a good space in that time she could have went into the store and finished her shopping. My sister she is so crazy she parks in a fire lane to go the ATM and she has been ticketed twice. I am smarter I Just take the first spot I can find, close or not. I walk the extra few step to the store or movies or bank. Then Im on my way while other people are still circling the parking lot, looking for a good space. Enjoy the extra exercise too.

---

[1] Citizenship and Immigration Canada. (2008, June 13). About Us. Retrieved November 24, 2008, from http://www.cic.gc.ca/english/department/index.asp

CHAPTER 3: ILLUSTRATION

Eliminating Details That Don't Fit

Below are topic sentences and lists of supporting details. Put an **X** by the details that do not fit the topic sentence.

a. topic sentence: An unreasonable boss can make a worker's job difficult.

_____ Some bosses may lose their tempers without warning.
_____ The worker is always on edge.
_____ Other supervisors may suddenly change the rules.
_____ They won't listen to questions or appeals.
_____ The worker is left to follow a foolish rule.
_____ Bosses get paid more than most workers.
_____ Some managers take an instant dislike to a worker.
_____ They might persecute that worker.
_____ Bosses should not be allowed to leave early if workers can't.

b. topic sentence: People are increasingly treating public spaces as private ones.

_____ I've seen women applying makeup on the subway.
_____ Subways are efficient means of transportation.
_____ Business people hold meetings in local coffee shops.
_____ Public cell phone conversations often include intimate details.
_____ Wireless Internet service allows people to check e-mail and do their banking in public spaces, often with strangers looking over their shoulders.
_____ I would never do my banking online.
_____ Couples often fight in public.

c. topic sentence: Certain foods are associated with religious celebrations.

_____ Honey is used in dishes to celebrate Passover.
_____ Home cooks often bake gingerbread for Christmas.
_____ Gingerbread houses are tedious to make.
_____ Oranges and whole fish are often present during Chinese New Year celebrations..
_____ My family eats *sheera* on the first day of Diwali. .
_____ *Latkes* are probably my family's favourite Chanukah food.
_____ *Mithai*, or milk-based sweets, are often eaten at Eid.
_____ Many children associate Easter with the Easter bunny.

CHAPTER 3: ILLUSTRATION

Revising Long Sentences

Students often include too many ideas in one sentence. The following sentences taken from student writings are long and rambling. Read each sentence carefully for its ideas. Then divide it into two separate and complete sentences.

1. This article relates to business because the 3-D theatre is losing profits and throughout the years it has not been in demand even though they are trying to make Hollywood action movies into 3-D so that people will come see it more often.

   _____

   _____

   _____

2. Because there is so much free online information and we're in a computer age, people are reluctant to purchase hard copies of encyclopaedias although Microsoft's Encarta software has been a best seller.

   _____

   _____

   _____

3. As a result of the bird flu scare, supermarkets and fast-food chain sales have slumped and they might have potential layoffs and millions of small farmers are losing a valuable source of income as their poultry is slaughtered.

   _____

   _____

   _____

4. The Baby Boomers are investing in larger homes, rather than retiring to small units, resulting in less inheritance for their children but more furniture sales for retailers.

   _____

   _____

   _____

CHAPTER 4: DESCRIPTION

Identifying Sentences That Are Too General

Below are lists of sentences. Put an **X** by one sentence that is general and vague in each group.

a. 1.   I like to live life to the fullest.

    2.   I enjoy adventures like sky diving and rock climbing.

    3.   I like to spend my free time volunteering at the hospital and at the Boys' and Girls' Club.

b. 1.   The city streets were jammed with people pushing their way to offices and stores.

    2.   The city was full of the hustle and bustle of urban life.

    3.   Horns blared and cars squeezed past one another on the city streets.

c. 1.   He kept fidgeting with his tie.

    2.   He was biting his nails.

    3.   He seemed anxious.

d. 1.   The bathroom counter was covered with open jars and hardened toothpaste.

    2.   The bathroom was a mess.

    3.   Wet towels draped over every surface in the bathroom.

e. 1.   The children's teacher greeted them with a big smile.

    2.   The children's teacher gave each child a pencil and sang a welcome song.

    3.   The children's teacher was friendly and kind.

CHAPTER 4: DESCRIPTION

Writing Sense Descriptions

Write sense descriptions for the items below.

a. Write three words or phrases to describe the taste of curry.

1. _____
2. _____
3. _____

b. Write three words or phrases to describe the texture of a sandy beach.

1. _____
2. _____
3. _____

c. Write three words or phrases to describe a park just after a snowfall.

1. _____
2. _____
3. _____

d. Write three words or phrases to describe the sounds of the campus cafeteria at lunchtime.

1. _____
2. _____
3. _____

e. Write three words or phrases to describe the smells of a carnival.

1. _____
2. _____
3. _____

CHAPTER 4: DESCRIPTION

Putting Details in Order

Below are lists. Each list starts with a topic sentence. The details under each topic sentence are not in the right order. Put the details in logical order, with **1** being the first detail, **2** the second, and so forth.

a.   topic sentence: The first birthday dinner I cooked for my wife was a disaster. (Arrange the details from appetizer to dessert.)

     _____   The chocolate cake split in half as I carried it to the table.

     _____   The lighted birthday candles tumbled into the split and onto the floor.

     _____   I forgot to defrost the shrimp cocktail, so they were as hard as rocks.

     _____   I left the steaks in the broiler too long.

     _____   I tried to save the steaks by scraping off the cindery parts.

b.   topic sentence: Her outfit must have cost a fortune. (Arrange details from head to foot.)

     _____   Around her neck was a diamond choker.

     _____   Diamond earrings the size of dimes gleamed in her ears.

     _____   Elegant black pumps with red soles were on her feet.

     _____   Her skirt was perfectly tailored.

     _____   She carried an expensive designer clutch.

CHAPTER 4: DESCRIPTION

Revising a Paragraph for More Specific Details

In the paragraphs below, the details that are underlined are not specific. Change the underlined sentences to a more specific description. Write the changes in the lines below each paragraph.

a. The honours ceremony was solemn and dignified. The stage was decorated with a forest of potted palms and dark blue velvet chairs. The front of the podium was covered by a glittering disk of the seal of the college. The faculty procession began the ceremony as the professors in their black academic robes and colourful hoods filed into their seats. Then the students came in. They looked good in their caps and gowns. They walked in looking very serious. An organist played a slow march as the students took their seats.

revisions: _____

_____

_____

_____

b. The florist's shop invited me to buy something. Every corner of the room was filled with colour. There were waxy pink-and-white tulips, buttery yellow daffodils, and deep purple violets. The scent of roses and carnations wafted from a beautiful arrangement waiting to be delivered. On the refrigerated shelves were many large and small arrangements. They were all different and very pretty. Tubs of cut flowers covered the floor.

revisions: _____

_____

_____

_____

CHAPTER 4: DESCRIPTION

Correcting Errors in Final Lines

Proofread the paragraph below, looking for errors in spelling, punctuation, mechanics, and word choice. Correct the errors by crossing out each mistake and writing the correction above it.

My bicycle ride through Tudor Woods was an escape into a natural haven. The narrow country roads was fringed by tall pine trees, and the trees created a dark, dense enviorment. Ridding under the canopy of trees, I smelled the green smell of pine needle's I felt the crunch of pine cones under the bike's wheels. No one were there accept me and the creatures of the woods. The squirrells were no afraid of me. They just stoped and stared at me as I rode by. Several blue jays dipped and swooped close to my face. Maybe they were curius. In one place, I saw owl sitting high in a tree he seemed mysterious and calm. The woods were a tranquil and beautiful retreat for me. They show me a different world from my bussy city life.

CHAPTER 5: NARRATION

Writing the Missing Topic Sentences in Narrative Paragraphs

Below are three paragraphs. If the paragraph already has a topic sentence, write that sentence in the lines provided. If it doesn't have a topic sentence, create one. (Two of the paragraphs have no topic sentence.)

a.   My daughter Suzanne and her friend Katie were bored. It was a hot day at the end of summer vacation, and the girls had nothing to do. "Why don't we open a lemonade stand?" I suggested. "What's that?" they asked. I explained that, in the old days, neighbourhood children used to set up little booths and sell cold lemonade by the glass. Suzanne and Katie thought it sounded like fun. They mixed up some powdered lemonade while I set up a card table in our front yard. Soon the girls were seated by the table, hoping for lots of business. The first people who came were very friendly adults, but they didn't have any money with them. Soon, two neighbourhood children spied the lemonade, raced home for money, and became the first customers. By the end of the afternoon, Suzanne and Katie had sold six glasses of lemonade and met many local children.

If the paragraph already has a topic sentence, write it here. If it doesn't, create one.

_____

_____

b.   A bad experience at work led me to discover my dog's capacity for sympathy. Last week, I had a terrible day at work. It started when I got in twenty minutes late and missed an important call from a customer with a complaint. Since the customer hadn't been able to get me, he had called my boss instead. My boss was furious with me both for not handling a customer's complaint and for being late to work. She put me on probation at work. The probation upset me, but I was more upset with myself for disappointing my boss, who had shown faith in me by hiring me. By the time I got home that night, I was depressed and discouraged. As I opened my apartment door, Casey, my Brittany spaniel, raced to greet me. She jumped to my knees as I stooped to pet hers. Suddenly she stopped jumping and looked into my face. Casey must have read my mind, for she began to lick my face. Her eyes looked sympathetic and concerned.

If the paragraph already has a topic sentence, write it here. If it doesn't, create one.

_____

_____

c.   I always thought Cameron was shy. Then, last night, he and I went to a club. The place was having a talent contest, and we watched as various singers and dancers performed for the audience. After about a half hour of watching, Cameron said, "I can do better than those people," and suddenly he was on stage. He sang like a professional. I was more surprised by his confidence than I was by his talent. He showed no fear of the crowd but acted as if he'd been singing for years. He smiled at people in the audience and strutted across the stage. He leaned across the edge of the stage, flirting with the ladies. When he finished singing, this supposedly shy man accepted the applause like a celebrity.

If the paragraph already has a topic sentence, write it here. If it doesn't, create one.

_____

_____

CHAPTER 5: NARRATION

Distinguishing Good Topic Sentences from Bad Ones in Narration

Below are sentences. Some would make good topic sentences for a narrative paragraph. Others would not: they are too big to develop in a single paragraph, or they are so narrow they can't be developed, or they make no point about an incident or incidents. Put an **X** by the sentences that would not make good topic sentences.

a. _____ I got my first Valentine when I was five years old.

b. _____ My first year in college was difficult for me.

c. _____ Taking the driving test turned into a comedy of errors.

d. _____ I had a bad car accident last week.

e. _____ My father showed real generosity when he stopped to help a homeless person.

f. _____ The anniversary party was held at a nightclub.

g. _____ Locking myself out of my car made me feel stupid.

h. _____ Thanksgiving dinner with my family taught me the meaning of patience.

i. _____ My time in the army gave me discipline and determination.

j. _____ I knew what it is like to be lonely when my best friend excluded me from his birthday party.

k. _____ My sister and I went to samba lessons last week.

l. _____ Marta learned patience when she worked as a nanny last summer.

m. _____ I discovered the meaning of friendship at a soccer game.

n. _____ Getting lost in the woods yesterday tested my courage.

o. _____ Larry and I had an encounter with a stray dog last night.

CHAPTER 5: NARRATION

Developing a Topic Sentence from a List of Details

Below are two lists of details. Each has an incomplete topic sentence. Read the details carefully; then complete each topic sentence.

a.   topic sentence: After I joined in a gossip session, I felt like a ———————

_____

      details: I have two friends who love to gossip.
                    When they gossip, they criticize.
                    Yesterday, they started talking about a man we knew in high school.
                    The talk got meaner and meaner.
                    Soon, they looked at me.
                    I was silent.
                    I didn't want to join in the gossip.
                    They started to make fun of me.
                    To stop them, I started to gossip too.
                    I said many things I regret.
                    I did it out of fear.

b.   topic sentence: Ever since my neighbour's apartment was robbed, I am _____

_____

      details: I always left my apartment door unlocked when I went to check the mail or to use the laundry room.
                    Last week, my neighbour's apartment was robbed.
                    First, she saw her door left open.
                    She entered cautiously.
                    On entering, she saw her furniture was ripped apart.
                    Then she saw her TV was missing.
                    Finally she checked her bedroom drawers.
                    She lost all her jewellery.
                    Her savings of $200 were gone.
                    Now I lock my apartment every time I leave it.

CHAPTER 5: NARRATION

Finding Details That Are Out of Order in a Narrative Outline

The outlines below have details that are out of order. Put the details in the correct order by numbering them, **1** for the detail that should be first, and so on.

a.   topic sentence: I'll never forget the day my son lost his tooth.

    details:

- _____ That night, as he placed the tooth under his pillow, he said, "I hope the tooth fairy doesn't forget to come this time".
- _____ He had a tennis lesson the day his tooth fell out.
- _____ He returned to the court, and not a minute later, the tooth was lying on the ground.
- _____ As he ran to hit a shot, he bit down on his tooth.
- _____ .His top tooth had been loose for days, and that morning he was wiggling it with his finger.
- _____ The tooth started to bleed so much I had to take him to the washroom and out his mouth.
- _____ I put the tooth in my wallet for safekeeping.

b.   topic sentence: My visit with my nephew made me feel ignorant.

    details:

- _____ I had to admit my ten-year-old nephew knew more about computers than I did.
- _____ My nephew wanted to show me his new computer.
- _____ He smiled when I suggested we play some computer games.
- _____ Instead of games, he went right to his e-mail.
- _____ His e-mail showed he corresponds with several people.
- _____ After checking his e-mail, he started to cruise through the Internet.
- _____ I laughed at his e-mail and said he must have several kids to correspond with.
- _____ He told me his correspondents are kids <u>and</u> adults.
- _____ He was highly skilled in searching the Internet.

CHAPTER 5: NARRATION

Recognizing Transitions in a Narrative Paragraph

Underline the transitions in the paragraph below.

A visit to my father's workplace helped me understand him. Before my visit, I considered my father an irritable man. Every night he would come home snarling and snapping. Then I saw where and how he worked. The first thing I noticed about his workplace was the noise. Several people talked at once, and they all spoke loudly. Meanwhile, phones were ringing. As soon as my father walked in, someone shouted, "Jim! Over here! We need you!" He rushed to help. Next, a different person called, "Jim! Come on! I need you to show me how to work this machine." At the same time, my father picked up a ringing telephone. "Let me put you on hold for one second," he said. The pressure and pace continued until closing time. Finally, my exhausted father, the last to go home, packed up and left. I was exhausted just from watching him. Now I understand why he might come home tired and cranky.

CHAPTER 5: NARRATION

Correcting the Errors in Final Lines

Proofread the paragraph below, looking for errors in spelling, punctuation, mechanics, and word choice. Correct the errors by crossing out each mistake and writing the correction above it.

I will never forget my first day at college. Although I hadn't got much sleep the

night before, I still wake before my alarm go off in the morning. I am feeling very

excited and anxious when I arrived at the college campus there were so many people

walking the halls. I soon got lost. However, student volunteers was wandering the

hallway's and one offered to help me. I have found my class with a few minutes to spare.

I felt even more nervous when I looked around the classroom and found that I was

probably the oldest student their. Then the professor walked and said "good morning."

The class did an introductory exercises and I learning the names of all my classmates

many were in the same program as me. I felt my nervousness ease. My other classes was

similar and by the end of the day I made some friends. I am now at the end of my first

semester and I am so happy I decided to come to college I would recommend it to

anyone.

CHAPTER 6: PROCESS

Recognizing Good Topic Sentences for a Process Paragraph

If a sentence is a good topic sentence for a process paragraph, put OK on the line provided. If a sentence has a problem, label that sentence with one of these letters:

A This is an announcement; it makes no point.
B This sentence covers a topic that is too big for one paragraph.
S This sentence describes a topic that does not require steps.

a. _____ Jasmine has a cheap, clean method for flushing the radiator of her car.

b. _____ My accounting teacher gave me a few helpful hints for living within a budget.

c. _____ The steps to success in your college career are easy to follow.

d. _____ How to find a good used computer will be discussed in this paper.

e. _____ A few simple steps showed me how to make exercise a valued part of my day.

f. _____ I have several tips on how to resist tempting snacks.

g. _____ Tom put himself through a rigorous programme of retraining to conquer his habit of oversleeping.

h. _____ The stages of a child's development track physical and mental growth.

i. _____ Movies are marketed in an elaborate process.

j. _____ Finding a good smart phone can be simple if you do a little research.

k. _____ The process of preparing the perfect espresso is the topic to be discussed.

l. _____ You can make delicious curry at home if you're willing to spend the time.

CHAPTER 6: PROCESS

Revising the Order of Steps in a Process Outline

The steps in each of these outlines are out of order. Put numbers in the spaces provided, indicating what step should be first, second, and so forth.

a.   topic sentence: My boyfriend pulls the same routine on me every weekend.

   _____   He calls up at 9 p.m. on Friday, saying, "You want to do something?"
   _____   I spend Thursday expecting him to call.
   _____   Every Wednesday, he says, "You want to go out on Friday? I'll call you and set it up."
   _____   All Friday morning, I wait for him to call me at work.
   _____   On my lunch hour on Friday, I check the movie listings in the paper.
   _____   By the time I get out of work on Friday, I am really irritated he hasn't called.
   _____   I am always a sucker and go out with him on Friday, after his last-minute call.

b.   topic sentence: Dominic has a system that saves him a fortune at the supermarket.

   _____   He waits until the store has a double coupon day.
   _____   On double coupon day, he uses as many coupons as he can.
   _____   He scours the Sunday papers for coupons.
   _____   He cuts out all the coupons for products he uses.
   _____   He files them, according to their expiration dates, in a little box.
   _____   As he leaves the store with his savings, he checks the bulletin board for the coupon exchange, planning new savings.

c.   topic sentence: My day just doesn't seem right if I don't follow my morning routine.

   _____   I have to drag myself out of bed and brush my teeth and wash my face.
   _____   Time to fight rush hour traffic!
   _____   Into the shower I go.
   _____   Time to figure out what to wear.
   _____   I grab a cup of coffee before I head out the door.

CHAPTER 6: PROCESS

Revising Transitions in a Process Paragraph

The transitions in this paragraph could be better. Rewrite the underlined transitions, directly above each one, so that the transitions are smoother.

Richard has a foolproof system for ironing his cotton dress shirts. First he makes sure the iron is on "Steam" and the steam section is filled with water. <u>Then</u> he carefully irons the collar, making sure no fabric wrinkles near the seams. <u>Then</u> he fits each shoulder around the end of the ironing board and irons the shoulders and top of the sleeves. <u>Then</u> he irons the main part of the shirt, from shoulder to bottom edge, very slowly. <u>Then</u> he irons the part around the buttons. He is careful not to burn the buttons by ironing on top of them. <u>Then</u> he does the sleeves and <u>then</u>, the cuffs. When he is finished, he has a professional looking shirt.

CHAPTER 6: PROCESS

Correcting Errors in Final Lines

Proofread the paragraph below, looking for errors in spelling, punctuation, mechanics, and word choice. Correct the errors by crossing out each mistake and writing the correction above it.

Chris knows exactly how to get away with bein late for the math class. First of all, he allways look very apologetic when he comes in late. He is whispering, "Excuse me and he slinks past the teacher. Then Chris creeps to the back of the room on tiptoe, and he silently take a desk in corner. All threw class, he looks humble and distressed. At the end of class, he is waiting untill all the other student's left the room. Finally, he approach the teacher. His eyes is tearful as he apologizes for being late. It never fails Chris always gets away with his rude behaviour.

CHAPTER 7: COMPARISON AND CONTRAST

Writing Appropriate Transitions for a Comparison or Contrast Paragraph

Decide whether each pair of sentences below shows a comparison or contrast. Then combine the two sentences into one, using an appropriate transition (a word or phrase). You may have to rewrite parts of the original sentences to create one smooth sentence.

a. MuchMusic presents many videos of currently popular songs.
    MuchMoreMusic shows a variety of classic videos.

    combined: *MuchMusic presents many videos of currently popular songs; on the other hand, MuchMoreMusic shows a variety of classic videos.*

b. My sister has a talent for singing.
    My mother is a gifted member of a community drama group.

    combined: _____

    _____

c. Going to the movies can cost as much as thirteen dollars a person.
    Renting a video can cost five dollars for a whole family.

    combined: _____

    _____

d. Keeping a journal is an outlet for your emotions.
    You can express your feelings by writing poetry.

    combined: _____

    _____

e. My studio is an organized environment.
    My house is a chaotic place.

    combined: _____

    _____

f. My sister is a brilliant mathematician.
    I am lost when it comes to numbers.

    combined: _____

    _____

CHAPTER 7: COMPARISON AND CONTRAST

Finding Differences in Subjects That Look Similar

Below are pairs of subjects that seem very similar but that do have differences. List three differences for each pair.

a. driving a car and driving an SUV

       differences: 1. _____

                          2. _____

                          3. _____

b. English class in high school and English class in college

       differences: 1. _____

                          2. _____

                          3. _____

c. reading for pleasure and reading for an assignment

       differences: 1. _____

                          2. _____

                          3. _____

d. frozen pizza and take-out pizza

       differences: 1. _____

                          2. _____

                          3. _____

e. living in an apartment and living in a house

       differences: 1. _____

                          2. _____

                          3. _____

CHAPTER 7: COMPARISON AND CONTRAST

Writing Topic Sentences for Comparison or Contrast

Below are lists of details. One list is for a comparison paragraph; the other is for a contrast paragraph. Read each list carefully; then write a topic sentence for each pair of lists.

a.   topic sentence: _____

_____

details

writing a letter	making a phone call
takes time to plan, write, edit and proofread	less time, can be done quickly and easily
materials: paper, envelope, stamp	need just a telephone
impact: leaves something permanent for reader to read again, for good or bad	once conversation is over, nothing remains

b.   topic sentence: _____

_____

details

writing a letter	making a phone call
contact: writer communicates at a distance	speakers don't see each other; they are separate
purpose: can convey news, business, or emotions	can be a business or personal call
expense: cost of stationery and a stamp is small	charge for a phone call is not expensive

31

CHAPTER 7: COMPARISON AND CONTRAST

Correcting the Errors in Final Lines

Proofread the paragraph below, looking for errors in spelling, punctuation, mechanics, and word choice. Correct the errors by crossing out each mistake and writing the correction above it.

   Unlike my first job, my current job is exhausting, demanding, and stressful. I got my first job informally, when I was twelve. My Aunt Raquel was moving out of her apartment, and she need help with packing and loading boxes into a rented truck. She said she pay me tweny dollars for helping her one Saturday. She worked beside me, and we took breaks whenever we felt tired. We played the radio and danced from box to box. All in all, it was an enjoyable way to earning twenty dollars. Today I work at a fast food restarant where I am on my feet all day. I work eight-hour shifts and almost never have time to take a brake. My manager is always checking up on me, insisting that I work faster. Sometimes he say's I am not friendlier enough to the custumers, I am being constantly nervous because I imagine the manager is standing behind me, waiting to criticize. At the end of my shift, I long for the time when I was a twelve year old moving person.

CHAPTER 8: CLASSIFICATION

Finding Categories That Fit One Basis for Classification

In the lines under each topic, write three categories that would fit the basis of classification given. The first one is done for you.

a.   topic: hats
     basis for classification: why they are worn
     categories:

1.   *hats worn to keep the wearer warm*

2.   *hats worn to protect against the sun*

3.   *hats worn to look stylish*

b.   topic: marriages
     basis for classification: how long they last
     categories:

1.   _____

2.   _____

3.   _____

c.   topic: computers
     basis for classification: what people use them for at home
     categories:

1.   _____

2.   _____

3.   _____

d.   topic: clothes
     basis for classification: for what special occasions they are worn
     categories:

1.   _____

2.   _____

3.   _____

CHAPTER 8: CLASSIFICATION

Combining Sentences for a Better Classification Paragraph

The paragraph below has some short sentences that would be more effective if they were combined. Combine each group of underlined sentences into one sentence. Write the new sentence in the space above the old ones.

I can classify my books by their place in my room; there are books on the desk,

books on the bookcase, and books on my night table. The books on my desk are my

schoolbooks. They are the books I need to read as soon as I can. <u>There is my Algebra I</u>

<u>book. I also have my Introduction to Public Speaking book. And then there's the book</u>

<u>for my Art Appreciation class.</u> These books are neatly stacked in a prominent place, but I

tend to avoid them because they represent the hard work I have to do. The books in my

bookcase are books I've acquired over the years. They are books I will read someday.

<u>They include biographies. There are also classics. One classic is *Two Solitudes*. An</u>

<u>English teacher recommended it to me.</u> These books are stacked up, but there are so

many books, the stacks are beginning to fall over. The last kind of book is the kind on

my night table. I read one of these books every night. They are entertaining books like

mysteries or thrillers. <u>They are tumbling all over the night table. They tumble because I</u>

<u>keep piling up new books I can't wait to read.</u> All my books serve some purpose in my

life, but some volumes are more attractive than others.

CHAPTER 8: CLASSIFICATION

Correcting Errors in Final Lines

Proofread the paragraph below, looking for errors in spelling, punctuation, mechanics, sentence structure, and word choice. Correct the errors by crossing out each mistake and writing the correction above it.

My experience as a coffee drinker has led me to beleive that the coffee I drink can be classified according to the situation I'm in. There are the coffee I drink every morning on my way to work. Because I drink this coffee every day, I restrict myself to the cheap, sugar-filled caffeine fix that Canadians can finding on every street corner. These morning coffees are quick, cheap, and give me the boost I need to get my morning started.. It's not my favourite coffee, but it does the trick. By the late afternoon my energy starts to lag so it's time for another coffee if I'm lucky enough to be near a café that sells iced coffee drinks I'll get one. Even if it is winter. I will buy an iced coffee. The only problem is the price, with the price of an iced coffee I could buy lunch instead. Finally there is the coffee I like to drink after dinner. After a fancy dinner out there's nothing like a latté after dessert. This latté might cost me double what one would cost in my local store but its worth it. When I think of all the difrent coffees I buy I realize I could probably buy a small car I figure that I need a treat now and then.

CHAPTER 9: CAUSE AND EFFECT

Creating Causes or Effects for Topic Sentences

For each of the following topic sentences, create three causes or effects, depending on what the topic sentence requires. The first one is done for you.

a.   topic sentence: I had several motives for starting an exercise program.

    1.   *I wanted to look better.*

    2.   *I wanted to get in shape for basketball.*

    3.   *My doctor told me I needed to lose weight.*

b.   topic sentence: Parents may impose curfews on teens for a number of reasons.

    1.   _____

    2.   _____

    3.   _____

c.   topic sentence: Losing your wallet can have unpleasant consequences.

    1.   _____

    2.   _____

    3.   _____

d.   topic sentence: Reading to a child can improve the parent-child relationship.

    1.   _____

    2.   _____

    3.   _____

e.   topic sentence: Students can have many reasons for not submitting assignments on time.

    1.   _____

    2.   _____

    3.   _____

CHAPTER 9: CAUSE AND EFFECT

Making the Connections Clear

Below are ideas that are connected, but the connection isn't clearly explained. Rewrite each pair of ideas, making the connection clear.

a.   Some people feel insecure. Therefore, they buy clothes with designer labels.

rewrite: _____

_____

(hint: Do designer labels offer security and status? Or do insecure people <u>think</u> designer labels convey status?)

b.   Brittany has a hard time showing affection. Therefore, Matthew broke up with her.

rewrite: _____

_____

(hint: Did Matthew want Brittany to express her affection more openly? Is Matthew a person who needs quite a bit of affection?)

c.   I am on a budget. Consequently, I rent movies instead of going to the theatre.

rewrite: _____

_____

(hint: Even though you are on a budget, do you still love movies? Do you love them enough to want to spend your limited resources on them?)

d.   I never did much reading in high school. So I am having a hard time reading in college.

rewrite: _____

_____

(hint: Do college courses require a great deal of reading? Are you having trouble because you never learned how to read difficult material?)

CHAPTER 9: CAUSE AND EFFECT

Recognizing Transitions in Cause or Effect

Underline the transitions in this paragraph. The transitions may be words, phrases, or clauses.

I miss my old neighbourhood because it was familiar, friendly, and full of things to do. First of all, I grew up in that neighbourhood, and I knew every part of it. I could tell any stranger the location of the nearest convenience store or the closest pay phone. I knew which stores were running specials on soft drinks and which restaurants had the best fries. Secondly, my old neighbourhood was a friendly place. Everybody knew everybody else. On summer nights, people sat on their front stoops and talked to each other. My mother was always babysitting for the neighbour's children, or a neighbour was babysitting for us. People helped each other out. And most important to me, as a child, was all the activity in the neighbourhood. There was always somebody to play ball with or just to hang out with. An empty lot on the corner made a great playground, and the abandoned shell of a building made a great playhouse. Because there were so many children in the area, and such great spaces for hiding, plotting, fighting, and playing, every day was an adventure for me.

CHAPTER 9: CAUSE AND EFFECT

Correcting Errors in Final Lines

Proofread the paragraph below, looking for errors in spelling, punctuation, mechanics, and word choice. Correct the errors by crossing out each mistake and writing the correction above it.

Taking a class in Mandarin had unexpected results. While I took the class because it was required for my International Business program, I was surprised to find out that I am very good at learning a foreign langage I had the highest grade on the final exam, and my quiz average was excellent too. My success in mandarin have convinced me to take another Chinese-language course. Another result of my taking the class is my increased interest in Chinese customs and culture. I have begun to pay more attention to the cultural events in my community. I recently saw my first kung-fu movie it was great. In the evenings, I find myself searching the Internet for Chinese tourist attractions. The most exciting effect of my becoming a Mandarin student is my planned vacation. This summer, I am taking a trip to Beijing. I hope my Mandarin lessons will help me on my Chinese adventure? I never thought, a required class like Mandarin would introduce myself to a world of new people, places, and idea's.

CHAPTER 10: ARGUMENT

Recognizing Good Topic Sentences for an Argument Paragraph

Some of the topic sentences below are appropriate for an argument paragraph. Some are for topics that are too large for one paragraph, and some are for topics that would require research. Some are announcements. Some do not take a stand. Put OK next to the sentences that would work well in an argument paragraph.

a. _____ Illegal drugs are destroying our country.

b. _____ People over 75 cause so many accidents that they should be required to take a driving test every year.

c. _____ The many cyclists in Toronto would benefit from more dedicated bike lanes.

d. _____ Why we need a bike lane on Forest Road is the subject of this paper.

e. _____ The city should do something about parking fines.

f. _____ Day care is bad for children.

g. _____ The price of books in the campus bookstore is a problem.

h. _____ Our college needs a safe, all-night study area.

i. _____ Parents of small children should pay careful attention to child safety.

j. _____ This issue of a dress code for Miller Elementary School will be discussed in this essay.

k. _____ Second-hand smoke can kill you, so smoking should be illegal in all public places.

l. _____ We should take action regarding ATVs on the beach.

m. _____ Carlton Township must enforce its no littering law.

n. _____ The intersection at Pine Drive and Collins Street needs a four-way stop sign.

o. _____ We must eliminate violence from television.

CHAPTER 10: ARGUMENT

Distinguishing Between Reasons and Details

Below are two lists. Each has three reasons and details for each reason. Put Reason 1, Reason 2, or Reason 3 next to the reasons on each list. Then put Details for 1, Details for 2, or Details for 3 by the items that give details for each reason. There may be more than one sentence of details connected to one reason.

a.   point: Our city should get rid of all minor league hockey teams.

      _____   I have seen children who are trembling before a game.

      _____   Some children burst into tears if they miss a shot.

      _____   The coaches in minor league hockey are often too demanding.

      _____   The parents who attend minor league games can be aggressive and cruel.

      _____   One coach in my neighbourhood ridicules players who don't perform well.

      _____   One parent called a player an idiot.

      _____   A parent attacked a referee about a bad call.

      _____   The pressure hurts the children who play.

b.   point: The college should close the pub in the student centre.

      _____   The temptation to party often becomes too strong for some students to resist.

      _____   Others, like a friend of mine, practically live in the pub.

      _____   My brother dropped out of college because the pressure to socialize and drink hurt his grades.

      _____   The college pub has a superficial purpose: to encourage students to socialize.

      _____   Many students plan their week and visit the pub only on their nights off.

      _____   The student union offers many other social activities for students, activities that do not involve drinking.

      _____   Students who want to drink and party can find alternate pubs off campus.

      _____   College is for studying, not partying.

CHAPTER 10: ARGUMENT

Working with the Order of Reasons in an Argument Outline

Below are topic sentences and lists of reasons. For each list, put an **X** by the reason that is the most significant, the reason you would save for last in an argument paragraph.

a.   topic sentence: Parents should read to their pre-school children as often as possible.

     reasons: 1. —— Small children love to hear stories.
                2. —— The act of reading is fun for parents.
                3. —— Reading to children develops their mental abilities and leads to later academic success.

b.   topic sentence: Students should turn their cellphones off in class.

     reasons: 1. —— Talking on the phone gives you less time to complete assignments.
                2. —— A ringing phone is a distraction to other students.
                3. —— Using a cellphone in class is disrespectful to the professor.

c.   topic sentence: All college and university courses should include an online learning supplement..

     reasons: 1. —— These supplements allow students access to course material at any time.
                2. —— Online learning supplements such as WebCT and Blackboard are very popular.
                3. —— Discussions can be continued outside class.

d.   topic sentence: We must ban the insertion of perfume samples in magazines.

     reasons: 1. —— People allergic to perfume can have a life-threatening reaction to the samples.
                2. —— Many readers find the strong odours of perfume unpleasant.
                3. —— Perfume samples make the pages heavy and stiff.

CHAPTER 10: ARGUMENT

Combining Sentences in an Argument Paragraph

Some of the sentences in the paragraph below could be combined to create a smoother style. Combine each group of underlined sentences into one sentence. Write the new sentence in the space above the old sentences.

Almost every time I am on the road, I see someone driving. The driver is also using a phone at the same time. I believe we must outlaw the use of a phone while a person is driving. The driver who is talking on a phone makes it harder for me to drive. I have seen those who are talking and driving slip into another lane and even weave all over the road. When I am near such a driver, I have to be careful. I have to watch out for such erratic behaviour. Since the driver on the phone is not paying attention, I have to pay extra attention. Phone drivers create problems for themselves. They may be driving with one hand. They may be preoccupied by their conversations. Either way, they are likely to run into a tree or a wall. Worst of all, phone drivers create safety problems for others. Their carelessness can cause them to ignore a red light. Their carelessness can cause them to ignore a turn signal. They may be following too closely. They may not hurt themselves, but they may hurt others. I have nothing against phones in cars. I think they are wonderful safety devices—as long as drivers pull off the road to use them.

CHAPTER 10: ARGUMENT

Correcting Errors in Final Lines

Proofread the paragraph below, looking for errors in spelling, punctuation, mechanics, and word choice. Correct the errors by crossing out each mistake and writing the correction above it.

My college need a club specificaly designed for older students. Students who are thirty or over come to school feeling very anxious they are not sure they can do the work, and they think all the younger students are much smarter. Older students tend to fill lost and alone a club would wellcome them to college and put them at ease. In addition a club could help them with their special concerns. Students in their thirtys and fourties are different from students right out of high school. Many are parent's; some are grandparents. They may be more concerned with a college day care centre than with college social activities. They may wanting more job placement seminars than basketball games. Finally, a club for older students would give them power. If older students' work together, they can acheive much more then if they work alone. The club could campaign for campus child care facilities or better job placement. A club could be a way to make older students feel like their a real part of college life.

CHAPTER 11: WRITING AN ESSAY

Identifying the Main Points in the Draft of an Essay

Below is the roughlines draft of a four-paragraph essay. Read it, then reread it, and underline the thesis and the topic sentences in each paragraph and in the conclusion.

Last month I turned on the local news and heard that my area might be hit by an ice storm. As the day passed, the storm moved closer, and the temperature hovered around 0° Celsius. Still, I was not worried. I had never been through an ice storm, and I figured it would be just a big blizzard. Until I actually experienced an ice storm, I had no idea of the damage it could do.

Before the storm, I really didn't believe the warnings of the weather channel. When they talked about storing drinking water, I figured I would probably need enough water for a day, at the most. Although the broadcasters predicted bad power outages, I assumed I might lose power for a few hours but would probably be lucky enough to keep my electricity. All the talk about buying batteries, a generator, a portable radio, and canned food went right over my head. After all, I thought, how bad could an ice storm be? I reasoned that it would last less than twenty-four hours, so after that, things would go back to normal. I decided the weather forecasters were sensationalizing the storm, just to attract an audience. I thought the forecasters were being melodramatic when they advised people to stay at home and to stay off the streets.

Well, I stayed at home in the dark for twenty-four hours. When the storm was over, I came out of the wreckage and faced the reality of a killer ice storm. First of all, part of my roof had collapsed. All the windows at the back of the house were shattered. In the front yard, the tall fir trees had fallen across the driveway and were blocking the main road. My neighbourhood was without electricity for one week and water for three weeks. Two days after the ice storm, I had no water, no heat, and very little food. If it hadn't been for the armed forces' mobile kitchens and generators, I would not have survived.

I am slowly rebuilding my house and my life. I am thankful that I lost only things, not family or friends. Because of the storm, I did gain one thing: a more realistic view of what an ice storm can do. It was quite a picture.

CHAPTER 11: WRITING AN ESSAY

Writing a Conclusion

Below is a partial essay. It has everything except a conclusion. Read the essay, paying careful attention to the introduction, thesis, and topic sentences, which are underlined to help you identify the main points. After rereading the essay, write a concluding paragraph that is three or more sentences long.

Every year, around Thanksgiving, I start to notice television commercials for champagne and newspaper ads for New Year's Eve parties at local restaurants. When I walk through the mall in December, I see hundreds of dazzling party dresses moved to the front of each display window. Also in December, my friends at work start to talk excitedly about what they'll do for New Year's Eve. I used to be just as excited as they are. But I don't feel that way any more. <u>I think New Year's Eve is bound to be a disappointment because people have placed such high expectations on a single night.</u>

<u>Everybody is supposed to think of December 31 as a time to look ahead with optimism, but the end of the year makes me depressed.</u> First of all, the last part of the year forces me to remember all the things I started out to accomplish, like quitting smoking or getting a promotion at work, and I have to face the fact that I didn't achieve all I wanted during the year. Meanwhile, television is devoted to "Year in Review" shows that look back on the year's movies, sports, music, crime, or scandals. All these shows remind me of the terrible things that have happened during the year. At the same time, my insurance agent and three other businesses send me calendars, encouraging me to plan for the coming year. So I'm caught between considering last year's messes and this year's possibilities.

New Year's Eve is supposed to be a night to celebrate the possibilities of the future, but the celebrations can fall flat. <u>The media presents New Year's Eve as a night of wild and exciting parties, but I've never been to a party that matched the image.</u> I've been to quiet parties and loud parties, to big parties and small ones, but all of them seemed to have the same flaw. All the partygoers were hanging around, waiting for something special to happen. After all, it was New Year's Eve. It was supposed to be a special night, wasn't it? The only thing special that ever happened was that everybody kissed at midnight. Then everybody wondered what to do next.

<u>Probably the best New Year's Eve I ever had was the one where I had absolutely no plans.</u> I had been invited to a number of parties, but I just couldn't spare the cash at the time, and so decided to spend a quiet evening in with some takeout food and the local 'Countdown to New Year's' show on TV. I had just sat down with a slice of pizza and a beer when the phone rang; it was my sister, who said that her New Year's plans had fallen through. She asked if she could come over and spend the evening with me. Pizza's always better with company, so I told her to drop by. We had the greatest time: we talked about our boyfriends, gossiped about our friends, and complained about our

bosses. I wondered why I had never considered spending New Year's Eve with my sister before.

(Write a conclusion.) _____

_____

_____

_____

_____

CHAPTER 11: WRITING AN ESSAY

Correcting Errors in Final Lines

Proofread the paragraph below, looking for errors in spelling, punctuation, mechanics, and word choice. Correct the errors by crossing out each mistake and writing the correction above it.

"Accident Prone"

Some people get hurt in terrible accidents. They get hit by a car, or they fall from grate heights. I, on the other hand, get hurt in silly, stupid accidents. I can find an accident in the safest places.

One safe place where I manage to have an accident was the beach. I was by myself, taken advantage of a beautiful day by walking along the edge of the water. Suddenly I found the only hole in a flat, smooth beach. My foot hit the hole. I tripped and fall headlong on the sand. My face hit the only pebble on the beach and I chip my front tooth. On a perfect, sunny day, when the water was as flat as glass, I manged to have a beach accicent without even going into the water. Other people have boating injuries or beach volleyball injuries, but I had a beach walking injury.

My next injury occured at another unusual place, my desk in Business Math class. I was getting ready to turn in my homework, and I need to stapling the two sheet of problems. I pulled my tiny stapler from my backpack and tried to staple the homework. But my stapler jammed. In a panic, I tried to break open the parts of the stapler. Pounding the stapler against the top of my desk, a pencil was jammed into the stapler. All I got was a pencil with a broken point. In desperation, I stuck my finger into the jammed parts. The sections opened; then they snapped close again—around my finger! I was ashamed to be the only student injured while turning in his or her math homework.

I know that insurance companies sells special insurance for people with hazardous jobs. I wonder if they sell insurance for people like me. I need an insurance policy that covers hazards in safe places. Their the places where accidents seem to find me.

Quizzes and Extra Exercises for the Reading Selections

CHAPTER 2: Quiz on "A RIDICULOUS ADDICTION"

1. What "addiction" is this article about?

    _____

2. When Frank Bogley can't get a close spot, where does he park?

    _____

3. The local newspaper carried an account of a man charged with assault. Why did he assault someone?

    _____

4. How is the author's friend Lou the opposite of Frank?

    _____

5. The author and his friend Andy were late for an event because Andy was looking for a close spot. For what event were they late?

    _____

6. Where, according to the author, do the silliest parking duels take place?

    _____

Name three advantages (mentioned in the article) that come when a person gives up looking for a close spot.

7. advantage 1: _____

8. advantage 2: _____

9. advantage 3: _____

10. The author refers to a blue-haired lady in a Mercedes who does not pull out of her space. What does she do instead?

    _____

CHAPTER 2: Quiz on "THEY HOOT, HE SCORES"

1. Why is the Montreal Forum important to the high school hockey players?

    _____

2. Why are the hockey players feeling "intimidated and frightened"?

    _____

3. Describe the first mishap the author experiences.

    _____

    _____

4. What happens when the author tries to lose himself "in the group of players looping the rink"?

    _____

    _____

5. Describe the second mishap the author experiences.

    _____

    _____

6. What is the "fair trade-off," according to the author?

    _____

    _____

List four words or phrases the author uses to describe the noise of the hockey fans.

7. _____

8. _____

9. _____

10. _____

CHAPTER 3: Quiz on "STICKY STUFF"

1. What do the products and inventions discussed in the article "Sticky Stuff" have in common?

    _____

    _____

2. What did George De Mestral examine under a microscope?

    _____

3. *Velours* means "velvet" in French, and *crochet* means "small hook." Explain how the combination of the two words into *velcro* suits the new product.

    _____

    _____

4. List two uses of velcro fasteners.

    _____

5. What company originally developed adhesive tape and Post-it notes?

    _____

6. Compare Scotch tape and Post-it notes. In what way are the two products similar and in what way, different?

    similar _____

    different _____

7. As the authors state, the products listed in this article are "a powerful force for order." In what way is their statement both a fact and an exaggeration?

    *fact*_____

    exaggeration _____

CHAPTER 4: Quiz on "A PRESENT FOR POPO"

1. What relation is Popo to the author, Elizabeth Wong?

   _____

2. Popo could remember events that happened over twenty years ago but had trouble with her short-term memory. Name two things that Popo would easily forget.

   a. _____ *b* . _____

3. What could be seen through Popo's window?

   _____

4. What could be heard from her window?

   _____

5. What had Popo tied a ribbon to? What was its purpose?

   _____

6. Symbolically, what did Popo try to sweep away that might "be lurking on the walls"?

   _____

7. What caused Popo's death? How old was she when she died?

   a. _____ *b* . _____

8. Describe two features of the funeral procession that went through Chinatown.

   a. _____

   b. _____

9. How many relatives gather for the holiday feast on the Christmas following Popo's death?

   _____

10. What did the author's mother predict would happen "once the distribution of what was left of Popo's estate took place"?

    _____

CHAPTER 4: DESCRIPTION

Finding Sense Descriptions in "A Present for Popo"

In this portrait of her grandmother, Elizabeth Wong uses many descriptions that appeal to one or more of the five senses. Reread her essay, underlining as many words, phrases, or sentences of sense description as you find. Below, write the exact words of each description—word, phrases, or sentences—and write what sense(s) each appeals to.

a. description: _____

_____

sense(s) appealed to: _____

b. description: _____

_____

sense(s) appealed to: _____

c. description: _____

_____

sense(s) appealed to: _____

d. description: _____

_____

sense(s) appealed to: _____

e. description: _____

_____

sense(s) appealed to: _____

CHAPTER 5: Quiz on "One Caring Teacher Set Things Right"

1. Why does the narrator feel the need to write most in the morning?

    _____

    _____

2. What stereotypes did the narrator face as a young boy?

    _____

    _____

3. What assumptions were made about the narrator when he didn't initially succeed at school?

    _____

    _____

4. Until grade 3, what prevented the narrator from learning to write properly?

    _____

    _____

5. Accoring to Wagamese, what allows us to help other people?

    _____

    _____

CHAPTER 5: NARRATION

Recognizing Specific Details in "One Caring Teacher Set Things Right"

Vivid details make Wagamese's narrative effective. To become more aware of the details, complete this exercise. First, read the questions below; then reread "One Caring Teacher Set Things Right" looking for the answers. Complete the exercise by using Wagamese's exact words.

a.   Find three words or phrases Wagamese uses to describe the early morning:

     _____, _____, and _____

b.   Find three words or phrases that introduce the setting of the story:

     _____

     _____

     _____

c.   What is the thesis of the narrative?

     _____

     _____

d.   Write two sentences that describe the way the narrator felt i) entering the Bradford school for the first time, and ii) how he felt when his classmates laughed at him.

     _____

     _____

     _____

e.   Write the words or phrases that describe the narrator's writing before he received glasses.

     _____

     _____

CHAPTER 6: Quiz on "HOW TO GET A REFERENCE LETTER"

1. Why do educational institutions require reference letters?

   _____

   _____

2. Consider the sample 'reference letter' at the beginning of the article. What, according to the article, should the writer do differently?

   _____

   _____

3. What 'three pillars' are essential to preparing to get a good reference letter?

   _____

   _____

4. Why does Potter recommend not asking non-tenured faculty for reference letters? Give two reasons.

   _____

   _____

5. In addition to reference letters, what other items are often required by educational institutions?

   _____

6. Complete the following sentence: "Professors can only write you a good letter if

   _____ , _____ , and

   _____ .

CHAPTER 7: Quiz on "HEY, CANADA'S ONE COOL COUNTRY"

1. What form of comparison or contrast does Bennett use in this article?

    _____

2. What stereotypes of Canadians does Bennett present in the first paragraph?

    _____

3. What four political or social issues does Bennett contrast in the article?

    a. _____

    b. _____

    c. _____

    d. _____

4. According to Bennett, Canada's founders were more interested in

    _____ and _____ "than liberty and independence"

5. Does Bennett give the impression that she is impressed by Canada's social policies or not? Give examples to support your answer.

    _____

6. Bennett claims that Canadians are less religious than Americans; what does she consider is a consequence of this?

    _____

CHAPTER 8: Quiz on "I'M A BANANA AND PROUD OF IT"

1. *True or False (Circle one):* Wayson Choy is proud of being a "banana."

2. What does "banana" mean?

   _____

3. According to Choy, what made him a "banana"?

   _____

4. In spite of the discrimination they experienced in Canada, why did the Chinese of the late 19th century still prefer to immigrate to Canada than to remain in China?

   _____

5. What event changed the discriminatory attitudes towards the Chinese? Why?

   _____

6. In Chinese culture, why are formal names often replaced with nicknames?

   _____

7. What effect did assimilation have on the younger Chinese? On Choy himself?

   _____

8. What, according to Choy, is the struggle all immigrants face?

   _____

9. Choy states: "I accept the paradox of being both _____ and _____."

10. Choy claims the desire for _____ and _____ is universal.

CHAPTER 9: Quiz on "SAVING THE PLANET ONE SWAMP AT A TIME"

1.   Where was David Suzuki born?

     _____

2.   What effect did Suzuki's childhood swamp have on his view of the world?

     _____

     _____

3.   What seemingly positive effects might cause people to "shrug off global warming"?

     _____

4.   What two human actions have contributed to global warming?

     _____

5.   Suzuki names a number of effects higher global temperatures have had; name three of those effects.

     _____

6.   How is smog created?

     _____

7.   How will smog impact cities and people?

     _____

     _____

CHAPTER 10: Quiz on "HAVE WE FORGOTTEN THE TROJAN HORSE?"

1. What event marked the beginning of "the commercialization of just about everything"?

    _____

2. According to the *Globe*, "we are a culture as much defined by _____

    _____."

3. What would a legislated ban on corporate sponsorship violate?

    _____

4. What can we as individuals do?

    _____

5. About what record did the Ottawa city councillors question the Nike Corporation?

    _____

6. One school was recently offered equipment so that its students could watch 12-minute news broadcasts. What was the school offered?

    _____

    _____

7. Along with the 12-minute news broadcasts, what else will the students have to watch?

    _____

8. Instead of accepting corporate sponsorships, what does Charles Gordon suggest "wouldn't hurt"?

    _____

9. Why are corporations sensitive about their public image?

    _____

CHAPTER 10: Quiz on "ASSIMILATION, PLURALISM, AND 'CULTURAL NAVIGATION': MULTICULTURALISM IN CANADIAN SCHOOLS"

Read the following statements carefully. If the statement is true, circle T. If the statement is false, circle F.

T F   1. Multicultural assimilation means that participation in Canadian public life should foster a sense of common national heritage.

T F   2. A *paradigm* is a pattern of thought, a way to analyze a problem.

T F   3. The moral duty of all Canadian, according to pluralists, is to separate their public and private cultural obligations.

T F   4. Bilingualism and biculturalism apply only to French- and English-Canadians.

T F   5. *Hegemony* means a bitter quarrel or blood feud between different groups.

T F   6. Canadian students already have the freedom to celebrate and practise their cultural ancestry in the privacy of their homes.

T F   7. The 2001 Canadian census statistics reveal that more than 40% of the population in Brampton, Ontario, is of non-European or American descent.

T F   8. Most immigrants leave their ancestral customs and beliefs at the border when they enter Canada.

T F   9. Most ESL students receive more than enough English language training before they join mainstream academic courses in high school.

T F   10. *Demographics* involves the study of populations by statistics of birth, death, and disease.

CHAPTER 10: ARGUMENT

Completing an Outline of "Assimilation, Pluralism, and 'Cultural Navigation': Multiculturalism in Canadian Schools""

Hiren Mistry challenges the policy of assimilation in Canadian schools and argues that the idea is outdated and possibly dangerous. To understand the structure and supporting details of his essay, complete the following outline by using points from Mistry's essay.

I. Thesis: The differences between the assimilation and pluralism approaches to Canada's multiculturalism will leave a mark on our future.

II. Many established and powerful educators in Canada choose the assimilation paradigm.

   A. Participation in Canadian public life should foster a sense of common heritage.

   B. _____

   C. _____

III. Assimilationists promote common Canadian values because they fear differences.

   A. _____

   B. Exploring cultural ancestry will ghettoize students.

   C. _____

IV. The assimilationists' alarm is based on three factors.

   A. _____

   B. _____

   C. _____

V. Pluralist advocates promote the more global connections of Canadian students.

   A. _____

   B. _____

   C. Students need to learn how to interact with their multicultural peers in public space.

VI. Pluralists do not advocate an "either-or" scenario of cultural loyalties.

    A. _____

    B. _____

VII. The consequences of not promoting the pluralist approach to multiculturalism are manifold.

    A. Students will seek other ways to reinforce their personal and cultural identity.

    B. _____

    C. _____

VIII. Conclusion: Canadian educators must foster the cultural intelligence of their students and adopt a pluralist pedagogy to prepare them for life.

CHAPTER 11: Quiz on "WHEN IMMIGRATION GOES AWRY"

Read the following statements carefully. If the statement is true, circle T. If the statement is false, circle F.

T   F   1. According to the article, in 2020, cities will operate more or less the same way they do now.

T   F   2. Rankings of world cities show that the most liveable cities are relatively small.

T   F   3. Stoffman claims that Canada's immigration policies are doing 'irreparable harm' to its cities.

T   F   4. Canada's federal government has jurisdiction over urban affairs.

T   F   5. Canada's federal government has always explicitly stated its interest in rapid urban growth.

T   F   6. Up until the late 1980's, immigration intake was lowered from time to time.

T   F   7. Vancouver receives most of Canada's immigrants.

T   F   8. The United States is the country most comparable to Canada.

T   F   9. Poverty levels among immigrants are now much worse than among the Canadian-born.

T   F   10. According to the article, Canada should emulate Australia's immigration policy.

CHAPTER 11: Quiz on "JOINED IN JIHAD?"

Read the following statements carefully. If the statement is true, circle T. If the statement is false, circle F.

T   F   1. All Muslims in Islamic nations today automatically hate the West.

T   F   2. An *appellation* means a name or a title.

T   F   3. The current conflict in Iraq has brought many factions amongst Muslims closer together.

T   F   4. Peace and prosperity seldom reduce suspicion of other cultures and religions.

T   F   5. Racial profiling is just another form of stereotyping.

T   F   6. "Being in a state of flux" means the same as "being at the lowest point."

T   F   7. People in both the Islamic and Western worlds hold many misconceptions about each other.

T   F   8. According to the author Adnan Khan, no one can bridge the gap between the West and the Muslim world.

T   F   9. The conflict in Iraq was caused by political and economic factors, not religious differences.

T   F   10. *Internecine* warfare means conflict within a group.

Exercises for the Bottom Line: Grammar for Writers

THE BOTTOM LINE: A DIAGNOSTIC GRAMMAR TEST

In each pair of sentences below, one is correct. Put OK by the correct sentence.

a. 1. _____ We cooked a vegetarian casserole and served it at the family reunion.
    2. _____ We cooked a vegetarian casserole, and served it at the family reunion.

b. 1. _____ I loved the first *Matrix* movie but I didn't like any of the sequels.
    2. _____ I loved the first *Matrix* movie, but I didn't like any of the sequels.

c. 1. _____ The picnic was wonderful, then it started to rain.
    2. _____ The picnic was wonderful; then it started to rain.

d. 1. _____ When you see a yellow traffic light, you should slow down.
    2. _____ When you see a yellow traffic light you should slow down.

e. 1. _____ He missed the train because his alarm clock didn't go off.
    2. _____ He missed the train, because his alarm clock didn't go off.

f. 1. _____ My sister being a person who thinks for herself.
    2. _____ My sister is a person who thinks for herself.

g. 1. _____ The committee to select a chairperson tomorrow.
    2. _____ The committee plans to select a chairperson tomorrow.

h. 1. _____ I quit my job at the grocery store. Which turned out to be the best thing to do.
    2. _____ I quit my job at the grocery store, which turned out to be the best thing to do.

i. 1. _____ My favourite sports are swimming, mountain climbing, and playing golf.
    2. _____ My favourite sports are swimming, mountain climbing, and to play golf.

j. 1. _____ The crime watch committee decided to compile a list of volunteers, arrange a schedule of patrol hours, and assign each volunteer to a patrol time.

2. _____ The crime watch committee decided to compile a list of volunteers, arranging a schedule of patrol times, and assign each volunteer to a patrol time.

k. 1. _____ Building a nest, we saw two robins.
   2. _____ We saw two robins building a nest.

l. 1. _____ Slipping on the icy sidewalk, the books dropped.
   2. _____ Slipping on the icy sidewalk, I dropped my books.

m. 1. _____ My brother Jacob exercise nearly every day.
   2. _____ My brother Jacob exercises nearly every day.

n. 1. _____ She is so rude that it don't matter how politely I approach her; she will always be impolite.
   2. _____ She is so rude that it doesn't matter how politely I approach her; she will always be impolite.

o. 1. _____ Simon yelled at his partner, stamped his feet, and stormed out of the office.
   2. _____ Simon yelled at his partner, stamps his feet, and stormed out of the office.

p. 1. _____ If you had saved your money, you could have paid for the television.
   2. _____ If you would have saved your money, you could have paid for the television.

q. 1. _____ One of the girls from the top three schools is transferring to my class.
   2. _____ One of the girls from the top three schools are transferring to my class.

r. 1. _____ There is a Chinese restaurant and a cyber café on the corner.
   2. _____ There are a Chinese restaurant and a cyber café on the corner.

s. 1. _____ Somebody from the ladies' curling team left her shoes in the locker room.
   2. _____ Somebody from the ladies' curling team left their shoes in the locker room.

t. 1. _____ Ron told his father that his father's car needed a new battery.
   2. _____ Ron told his father that his car needed a new battery.

u. 1. _____ When I went to that bookstore, it was so crowded that you couldn't find anything.
   2. _____ When I went to that bookstore, it was so crowded that I couldn't find anything.

v. 1. _____ Jhumpha wants to ride to work with Maurice and I.
   2. _____ Jhumpha wants to ride to work with Maurice and me.

CHAPTER 12: THE SIMPLE SENTENCE

Recognizing Verbs

Underline the verbs in each of the following sentences.

a. In the morning, my brother and I prepared and packed a picnic lunch for the whole family.

b. The pavement was burning the soles of my feet.

c. The birds must have been a rare species from South America.

d. Children might accept the values of their peers.

e. Those cinnamon buns smell wonderful.

f. Adish appeared anxious about his job promotion.

g. Amanda was my best friend in high school.

h. Smoking can cause a number of serious illnesses.

i. Raheel will volunteer at Habitat for Humanity this summer.

j. My brother has been commuting between Hamilton and Toronto.

k. Sometimes Rolanda complains too loudly, irritates her boss, and loses the argument.

l. Some wrestlers are international celebrities.

m. Last week we lost an important match.

n. Regular exercise reduces your level of stress and burns calories.

o. The movie combines humour and suspense.

CHAPTER 12: THE SIMPLE SENTENCE

Recognizing Subjects

Underline the subjects in the following sentences.

a.   Yesterday, Rekha and Sanjiv were planning a wedding.

b.   Tomatoes might have been a better buy than corn.

c.   We had been collecting glass containers for recycling.

d.   At first, I drove very cautiously.

e.   Everything looked clean and shiny in the new apartment.

f.   Sometimes anger can lead to violence.

g.   Cereal and bananas covered the toddler's bib.

h.   Banks have changed their telephone banking services recently.

i.   Something has happened to the keyboard of my computer.

j.   Toddlers need a great deal of attention and care.

k.   Cooking and cleaning filled most of his weekend.

l.   Last night, mosquitoes bit me on my arms and legs.

m.   A squirrel is living in our attic.

n.   She and Nancy could have invited me to the family dinner.

o.   They can be very thoughtless at times.

CHAPTER 12: THE SIMPLE SENTENCE

Recognizing Prepositional Phrases, Subjects, and Verbs

Put parentheses around all the prepositional phrases in the following sentences. Then underline the subject and verb, putting *S* above the subject and *V* above the verb.

a.   In the back of my mind was a plan for a surprise party.

b.   One of my cousins is a law student at Dalhousie University.

c.   The toy inside the Cracker Jack box was a big treat for me.

d.   Over the years, the sisters grew closer and developed a bond of intimacy.

e.   Without a doubt, he deserved first place in the writing contest.

f.   From my point of view, the job is a big promotion for him.

g.   Two of my nephews are spending the weekend with me.

h.   A house without a basement is a waste of money.

i.   During the night, I must have lost an earring between the mattress and the headboard of the bed.

j.   At the bakery, we worked around the clock on holiday weekends.

k.   Under the circumstances, I can agree with you about the traffic ticket.

l.   The dog ran into the woods at the back of the house.

m.   John-David took a pen with a very fine point and sketched a figure.

n.   A cabin by the lake has been my dream house for years.

o.   The box on the counter is the one with the mail in it.

CHAPTER 12: THE SIMPLE SENTENCE

Finding Subjects and Verbs: A Comprehensive Exercise

Underline the subjects and verbs in these sentences, putting *S* above the subjects and *V* above the verbs.

a. Beyond the bike path is a beautiful lagoon with ducks and swans.

b. Haven't you considered a job in the construction industry?

c. George was hoping to graduate at the end of next year.

d. Within the family, my mother rarely talks about her job in the city.

e. Here are a your textbooks and memory stick for your first day at school.

f. You might have considered my feelings in your reorganization plan.

g. The man in the yard cut the lawn and trimmed all the bushes in two hours.

h. Did you ever try a drop of soy sauce on your chicken?

i. Dancing under the stars makes an evening special.

j. Among the wedding gifts was a silver bowl with a monogram of the couple's initials.

k. She and her mother designed a computer program for accountants and sold it to a major corporation.

l. One of the boys runs a small restaurant in town.

m. There is no real reason for alarm.

n. Joe has not called me in two months.

o. Either my mother or my sister will shovel the driveway.

CHAPTER 13: THE COMPOUND SENTENCE: COORDINATION

Recognizing Compound Sentences and Adding Commas

Add commas where they are needed in the following sentences.

a.   I expected a great performance but was disappointed in the famous guitarist.

b.   I've already called the repair service so you can just wait for its arrival.

c.   Parenthood is a very difficult role yet no one gets much training for it.

d.   Mountain climbing is a dangerous yet exhilarating sport for a few brave and hardy people.

e.   Olivia and Clarence faced each other across the table and negotiated a truce.

f.   Irving tried to apologize for his tardiness but Phil wasn't willing to listen.

g.   I had never eaten tofu before nor had I tasted yogurt.

h.   I asked for directions to the mall but neither my uncle nor my aunt could help me.

i.   Kim was pleasantly surprised by the audience for she had expected a much smaller crowd.

j.   The man ahead of me in line was shouting at the ticket agent and the man's wife was complaining loudly.

k.   They said they wanted their money back immediately or they would sue the company for fraud.

l.   I kept getting a busy signal for hours and finally gave up.

CHAPTER 13: THE COMPOUND SENTENCE: COORDINATION

Writing Compound Sentences 1

Combine each set of ideas into one compound sentence using a coordinating conjunction. Remember to insert a comma plus a coordinating conjunction between the related sentences.

1.   You have to work twice as hard as other people.
        You never learned the principles of organization.

        combined sentence: _____

        _____

2.   This seminar is not scheduled for your area.
        You might consider attending on-line.

        combined sentence: _____

        _____

3.   You can suffer an energy drain.
        You can finally learn how to cope with stress.

        combined sentence: _____

        _____

4.   Communication is the backbone of any effective team.
        You need more training in positive communications.

        combined sentence: _____

        _____

5.   Your once secure job goes into a tailspin.
        You need new skills to cope, adapt, and stay in control.

        combined sentence: _____

        _____

CHAPTER 13: THE COMPOUND SENTENCE: COORDINATION

Writing Compound Sentences 2

Combine each set of ideas into one compound sentence, using a conjunctive adverb. Remember to insert a semicolon, a conjunctive adverb, and a comma between the related sentences.

1.   You never learned the principles of organization.
        You have to work twice as hard as other people.

        combined sentence: _____

        _____

2.   This seminar is not scheduled for your area.
        You might consider attending on-line.

        combined sentence: _____

        _____

3.   You can suffer an energy drain.
        You can finally learn how to cope with stress.

        combined sentence: _____

        _____

4.   Communication is the backbone of any effective team.
        You need more training in positive communications.

        combined sentence: _____

        _____

5.   Your once-secure job goes into a tailspin.
        You need new skills to cope, adapt, and stay in control.

        combined sentence: _____

        _____

CHAPTER 14: THE COMPLEX SENTENCE: SUBORDINATION

Punctuating Complex Sentences

All the sentences below are complex sentences. Add a comma to the sentences that need one.

a.   If you want to go to the movies you have to get ready now.

b.   I have to buy fresh chocolate chip cookies whenever I pass that bakery.

c.   Since Reza has no interest in hockey I go to the games with my brother.

d.   Selena will tell us if she needs help with moving out of her apartment.

e.   While the cashier rang up his purchases Nitish searched for the correct change.

f.   My daughter will not go to sleep unless I sing her a lullaby.

g.   Before the couple moved to Alberta they spent some time in Manitoba.

h.   My father sits on a bench in the mall while my mother shops for bargains.

i.   When disaster strikes a community ordinary people become courageous and self-sacrificing.

j.   One crime can change an entire town because the fear of crime affects everyone.

k.   Unless we start saving money we'll never be able to afford a new car.

l.   There is a great deal of work to do in a restaurant before it opens its doors every day.

m.   Because traffic was backed up for miles I spent two hours sitting in my car last night.

n.   I will not relax until the semester is over.

o.   After you call me call the babysitter at home.

CHAPTER 14: THE COMPLEX SENTENCE: SUBORDINATION

Punctuating Simple, Compound, and Complex Sentences

Add the necessary punctuation (commas, or semicolons, or semicolons and commas) to the sentences below. Do not add words; just add punctuation. Some sentences need no punctuation.

a. As I reached for my cup I accidentally dipped my fingers into the hot coffee.

b. Lenore reread the manuscript carefully and eliminated any awkward phrases.

c. Mrs. Espinoza is a trained dietician however she prefers to work as a food columnist for the local paper.

d. Although my backyard is small it is landscaped with a variety of plants.

e. He started college as a business major then he decided to major in engineering technology.

f. Luc likes all kinds of music but his favourite is country music.

g. Cooking does not have to be a chore in fact it can be a pleasure.

h. I had rehearsed my speech several times thus I was not nervous during my presentation.

i. Al rushed to the airport but missed his flight by minutes.

j. You have to be committed to your job or you will never get ahead.

k. We had a hard, cold winter so we were overjoyed by the first signs of spring.

l. I was eager to move out consequently I grabbed the first apartment I saw.

m. When the days start to get longer I like to take a walk in the evening.

n. The little boy shot the puck as the crowd cheered wildly.

o. Even though I complain about my job I enjoy working with the public.

p. Until I started basic training in the armed forces I had never experienced the meaning of the term "discipline."

q. My older sister taught me table manners moreover she educated me about polite conversation.

r. Before the game started the coach gave the players a speech about sportsmanship.

s. The neighbours never spoke to us nor did they wave at us from their cars.

t. Education is a good investment it pays off throughout your lifetime.

CHAPTER 15: AVOIDING RUN-ON SENTENCES AND COMMA SPLICES

Correcting Run-On (Fused) Sentences

Some of the sentences below are correctly punctuated; some are compound sentences without the necessary commas. Others are run-on (fused) sentences. If the sentence is correctly punctuated, put **OK** in the space provided. If it is a run-on sentence or needs punctuation, put an **X** in the space and correct the sentence. To correct a sentence, you do not have to add words; just add the necessary punctuation.

a. _____ She tried to describe the accident but couldn't find the right words for the disaster.

b. _____ Mei sat through the movie without laughing once the comedy offended her instead of amusing her.

c. _____ Some of the most careful drivers can make mistakes on the road or become victims of reckless drivers.

d. _____ I dread getting up for work at 6 a.m. it is just too early for me to function.

e. _____ He was very nervous about taking Introduction to Public Speaking but he managed to do very well in the class.

f. _____ You should dress well at a job interview for your appearance is important to prospective employers.

g. _____ My husband packs the children's lunches every morning meanwhile, I get the children dressed for school.

h. _____ The phone rings every night at seven then a recorded message asks me to buy health insurance.

i. _____ Gambling can be a disease, but some gamblers don't want to admit they are addicted.

j. _____ My husband took me out to dinner for my birthday and he gave me a very expensive gift.

CHAPTER 15: AVOIDING RUN-ON SENTENCES AND COMMA SPLICES

Correcting Comma Splices

Some of the sentences below are correctly punctuated. Some contain comma splices. If the sentence is correctly punctuated, put **OK** in the space provided. If it contains a comma splice, put **X** in the space and correct the sentence. To correct the sentence, you do not need to add words; just correct the punctuation.

a. _____ Nothing ever happens in our town, we have no excitement, adventure, or thrills.

b. _____ Nothing exciting ever happens in our town, on the other hand, nothing tragic ever happens, either.

c. _____ My girlfriend is a great tennis player, and she's great at racquetball too.

d. _____ You can get a good deal on a car at Simmons Auto, however, you can get better financing at Lexington Honda.

e. _____ He promised to repay the loan by Friday, then on Friday he was nowhere to be found.

f. _____ Cereal makes a good breakfast, and it is a fairly cheap one.

g. _____ Introduction to Computers is a required course, moreover, it will be useful in your landing a good job.

h. _____ The house had been furnished by an interior decorator, yet the rooms seemed overcrowded and overdecorated.

i. _____ I finally completed Algebra I, next I tackle Algebra II.

j. _____ Sam wants to go to Acapulco next winter, so he is taking a class in Conversational Spanish this fall.

CHAPTER 15: AVOIDING RUN-ON SENTENCES AND COMMA SPLICES

Coordination: A Comprehensive Exercise

Add a comma, or a semicolon, or a semicolon and a comma to the following sentences. Don't add, change, or delete any words. Just add the correct punctuation.

a. I've finished cleaning the bathroom now I'll tackle the kitchen floor.

b. I have always dreamed of visiting my grandfather yet I've never saved enough money for the trip.

c. My cousins watch soap operas all day consequently their view of the world is somewhat distorted.

d. Murray is a generous person so I wasn't surprised by his donation to the children's shelter.

e. The library and the old high school are the oldest buildings in our neighbourhood and they are also the most beautiful.

f. He needs to grow up a little then he can think about enlisting in the armed forces.

g. Professor Sauer is a tough teacher nevertheless she is my favourite instructor.

h. I lost my driver's license thus I was unable to drive to work last week.

i. My mother made my favourite dessert last night so I paid her back by washing the dishes.

j. Toddlers are adorable on the other hand they demand a great deal of love and care.

k. I love to watch the eleven o'clock news but I'm usually sound asleep by ten.

l. I never took Basic Geometry in high school nor did I have to take Introduction to Statistics.

m. My sister is gifted in mathematics therefore she is considering a career in math education.

n. I expected my son to hate pre-school instead he enjoys it.

o. My parents taught me honesty my sister taught me kindness.

CHAPTER 16: AVOIDING SENTENCE FRAGMENTS

Checking Groups of Words for Subjects and Verbs

Check the following groups of words for subjects and verbs. Some have subjects and verbs; they are sentences. Some are missing subjects or verbs or both. They are fragments. Put an *S* by the ones that are sentences; put an *F* by the ones that are fragments.

a. _____ A clear example being the terrible condition of the road near the Quick Stop store.

b. _____ Not once in the history of twentieth-century Canadian society.

c. _____ Doesn't have any impact on the decision at all.

d. _____ Will have a great deal of influence on the outcome of the election.

e. _____ His argument was a good example of using the facts to make a point.

f. _____ The man rents the house across the street from the police station.

g. _____ My purpose to warn the homeowners of potential flaws in the electrical wiring.

h. _____ For example, you can save money by comparison shopping.

i. _____ In addition, a fine new cafeteria for the elementary school.

j. _____ Children lacking role models at home or in the community.

k. _____ Especially the widespread use of sugar substitutes like Nutra Sweet in soft drinks

l. _____ The Nelsons are living in my parents' apartment.

m. _____ Carrie gaining the strength and confidence to make it through her senior year.

n. _____ Believed all his life in the need for a strong family unit.

o. _____ The new employee to train with the more experienced people at his workplace.

CHAPTER 16: AVOIDING SENTENCE FRAGMENTS

Checking for Dependent-Clause Fragments

Some of the following groups of words are sentences; some are dependent clauses punctuated like sentences but are sentence fragments. Put an *S* by the sentences and an *F* by the fragments.

a. _____ While the music blared and the dancers crowded the floor.

b. _____ After the rain stopped its steady beating against the canvas tent.

c. _____ In the afternoon I do my assignments for the following week.

d. _____ The ragweed season is hard on my allergies.

e. _____ When the principal spoke to the graduating class of Central High School.

f. _____ Whether he finishes high school or drops out to work full time.

g. _____ Common sense is not that common these days.

h. _____ Because Adebola has a great sense of humour and an outgoing personality.

i. _____ If I can manage to save something from my salary every week.

j. _____ How you decide to spend the money from the sale of your car.

k. _____ Before the alarm goes off in the morning.

l. _____ Not everyone is suited to work in a restaurant.

m. _____ Sometimes he calls the office from his car.

n. _____ Where the stores sell fashionable clothes at reasonable prices.

o. _____ Since no one seemed to be interested in the subject of his lecture.

CHAPTER 16: AVOIDING SENTENCE FRAGMENTS

Correcting Sentence Fragments

All the groups of words below contain sentence fragments. Correct them in the most appropriate way.

a. Because I couldn't find a place to park. I gave up and drove home.

    corrected: _____

    _____

b. The man in the next booth arguing with his girlfriend about the price of her meal.

    corrected: _____

    _____

c. With my satellite dish, I can get any television station I want. Except the local network affiliates.

    corrected: _____

    _____

d. It is hard to concentrate on homework. When your neighbours are making noise.

    corrected: _____

    _____

e. I love the music at the Cabana Club. Especially the steel band on Wednesday evenings.

    corrected: _____

    _____

f. His purpose is to convince the Planning Council of the need for a playground. In the Victoria Hills district.

    corrected: _____

    _____

g. The school children on the field trip being under the supervision of a teacher and a teacher's aide.

corrected: _____

_____

h. Since he had lost his job last month and couldn't find another. Kevin was unable to make his car payment.

corrected: _____

_____

i. Mira wished for a three-day weekend. To catch up on her chores. To relax at the lake.

corrected: _____

_____

j. While Ruben is an outgoing and talkative person. His brother Edward is extremely shy.

corrected: _____

_____

CHAPTER 16: AVOIDING SENTENCE FRAGMENTS

Avoiding Fragments: A Comprehensive Exercise

Some of the following are complete sentences; some are sentence fragments. Put an *S* by the sentences and an *F* by the fragments.

a. _____ The reason for my lateness is a problem with my alarm clock.

b. _____ Without a chance for admission into the concert of the year.

c. _____ My cousin being a very talented designer of ceramic candlesticks and bowls.

d. _____ Because very few people are willing to give up their precious free time to attend a boring lecture.

e. _____ With a smile and a wave, he left the house.

f. _____ The reason being a childhood spent on a cold and isolated farm.

g. _____ Behind all the salesperson's claims of superior performance and state-of-the-art technology.

h. _____ Which took me completely by surprise and made me uncomfortable.

i. _____ The results of the vote to be announced at the annual meeting next week.

j. _____ Since the weather was warm and humid, the hikers wore shorts and T-shirts.

k. _____ For example, immigrants from countries such as Chile and Argentina.

l. _____ Before you spend all your money on a new truck with luxurious accessories, think again.

m. _____ Doesn't mean a single thing to me or you.

n. _____ The announcer with the loud, excited voice and the Scottish accent.

o. _____ Behind the gas station is a car wash.

CHAPTER 17: USING PARALLELISM IN SENTENCES

Revising Sentences for Parallelism

Some of the following sentences need to be revised so that they contain parallel structure. Revise the ones that need parallelism.

a.   I want a hamburger with onions and that has Swiss cheese.

   revised: _____

   _____

b.   I have stopped going to that club because the prices are too high, with rude and pushy customers, and the music is out of style.

   revised: _____

   _____

c.   After we had managed to rake the leaves and bagging them, they blew across the yard.

   revised: _____

   _____

d.   Working for yourself can be harder than working for someone else.

   revised: _____

   _____

e.   The recital started at nine; eleven was the time it ended.

   revised: _____

   _____

f.   The beauty of the prairie, its size, and the way it looked isolated made a lasting impression on me.

   revised: _____

   _____

g. Art is my most enjoyable class, in addition, the one that is most interesting and most presents a challenge.

   revised: _____

   _____

h. After the tour of the facilities, the guide gave a brief history of the clinic, showing a short video, and answering any questions.

   revised: _____

   _____

i. The camp counsellor was eager to get the children settled in, make them feel comfortable, and to distract them from their homesickness.

   revised: _____

   _____

j. Seeing the driver run a red light makes me feel angry, indignant, and not having any power.

   revised: _____

   _____

CHAPTER 17: PARALLELISM IN SENTENCES

Parallelism: A Comprehensive Exercise

Some of the sentences below are parallel in structure and are correct; others lack parallelism. Put an *X* by the sentences that need to be revised so that they have a parallel structure.

a. _____ When he arrived at the premiere, the star of the film looked glamorous, elegant, and rich.

b. _____ I am looking for an employee who wants to learn, is willing to work long hours, and with a desire to get ahead.

c. _____ It is never easy to apologize for an unkind remark or accepting an apology from an unkind person.

d. _____ Introduction to Canadian History, Environmental Conservation, and a course called Western Civilization are all challenging courses.

e. _____ Vadim is happier living in a small town than to fight the crowds in the city.

f. _____ After I received my diploma, I tossed my cap in the air, cheered loudly, and hugged my wife and children.

g. _____ Because Christopher took too many classes, was working long hours at the hotel, and spent too much time commuting, he had no time for his family.

h. _____ The child who witnessed the crime became silent, feeling anxiety, depressed, and distrustful.

i. _____ People who want to attend the concert can buy tickets in advance or at the gate.

j. _____ Over the years, he has held a variety of jobs as an electrician's helper, a limousine driver, a man who tends gardens, a waiter, and a bartender.

k. _____ If you enjoy people-watching, you can go to a park or beach, or a mall is a good place to go.

l. _____ The turning points in my life were my high school graduation, my enlistment in the armed forces, and my daughter's birth.

CHAPTER 18: CORRECTING PROBLEMS WITH MODIFIERS

Correcting Sentences with Misplaced and Dangling Modifiers

Some of the following sentences contain misplaced or dangling modifiers. Revise any sentence with a modifier problem.

a.   Stuck in a traffic jam at rush hour, an overheated engine was a real danger.

   revised: _____

   _____

b.   Slithering across the floor, I screamed when I saw the snake.

   revised: _____

   _____

c.   Last weekend my roommate and I nearly refinished the whole oak table.

   revised: _____

   _____

d.   As a tiny baby, the family made the dangerous journey across the continent.

   revised: _____

   _____

e.   After surviving Biology I, Biology II seemed like an easy course.

   revised: _____

   _____

f.   Before entering the restaurant, I had to take off my shoes and leave them in the hallway.

   revised: _____

   _____

g.   The driver of the tractor trailer ran into a concrete wall while exceeding the speed limit.

   revised: _____

   _____

h.   Under a great deal of pressure, the deadline was impossible to meet.

revised: _____

_____

i.   Lingering too long at the party, the parents were furious at their son for breaking his curfew.

revised: _____

_____

j.   Grabbing a sale item out of the hands of the shopper, a battle broke out.

revised: _____

_____

CHAPTER 18: CORRECTING PROBLEMS WITH MODIFIERS

Misplaced and Dangling Modifiers: A Comprehensive Exercise

Some of the sentences below are correct; some contain misplaced or dangling modifiers. Put an *X* by the sentences that have problems with modifiers.

a. _____ To work from home, high-speed Internet access is useful.

b. _____ While washing the kitchen floor, the contractor kept tracking mud on the linoleum.

c. _____ I hoped to donate some suits that didn't fit me to a thrift shop.

d. _____ Rolling around in the mud, Damita laughed at the piglets.

e. _____ When he finishes college, he wants only his family to attend his graduation.

f. _____ Armed with a search warrant, the police had every right to search the smuggler's apartment.

g. _____ The old church is bordered by a deep lake where I was married.

h. _____ Troubled by mysterious nightmares, she was afraid to sleep.

i. _____ Losing faith in the team, the player began to slacken his efforts.

j. _____ While talking on the phone, my dinner turned stone cold.

k. _____ He was taking the automotive class with a friend named Raheem.

l. _____ Christina stuffed the cookies she had not eaten into a plastic bag.

m. _____ I wanted a cake from the bakery that said "Happy Birthday" on it.

n. _____ We came home after a trip to Jamaica on Saturday.

o. _____ Sizzling on the grill, I checked my perfectly seasoned chicken.

CHAPTER 19: USING VERBS CORRECTLY

Picking the Correct Verb in the Present Tense

Underline the subject and circle the correct verb form(s) in each sentence below.

a.   Carlos and Adrian never clean/cleans their apartment.

b.   You confuse/confuses the child with your explanations.

c.   The man behind the counter smile/smiles at every customer.

d.   I memorize/memorizes the rules and repeat/repeats them before a test.

e.   They rarely consult/consults their family about money problems.

f.   From June to August, we search/searches for good places to swim.

g.   The boys in the neighbourhood distrust/distrusts strangers.

h.   You cause/causes trouble with your constant gossip.

i.   Truck with heavy loads damage/damages the surface of the road.

j.   A person's first paycheque bring/brings a feeling of pride.

k.   The baby in the nursery smile/smiles at me every day.

l.   Hidden anger cause/causes only trouble between friends.

m.   Orchids with mauve centres seem/seems the prettiest.

n.   Every winter, we put/puts the storm windows on the house.

o.   Tomatoes from your own garden taste/tastes better than tomatoes from the store.

CHAPTER 19: USING VERBS CORRECTLY

Using the Correct Verb in the Past Tense

Write the correct past tense verb form in the blank space.

a. A year ago, I _____ (sign) up for a walk-a-thon and _____ (raise) $400 for charity.

b. When we were friends in elementary school, we _____ (call) each other by nicknames.

c. The salesperson _____ (approach) me with an offer for a special discount on the entertainment unit.

d. Sylvia did her best, but her mother _____ (criticize) her for not winning the contest.

e. The crowd at last night's game _____ (roar) with approval when he _____ (score) the winning goal.

f. Before he took a class in English, he _____ (travel) with a Chinese-English dictionary.

g. After I graduated from high school, I _____ (respect) my toughest teacher.

h. Whenever she got a new stamp, she _____ (paste) it in her stamp album.

i. After I arrived at the emergency room, a police officer _____ (confirm) that my brother had been injured in an accident.

j. Last night, Jameel _____ (ask) me about going into business together.

k. Before I moved out of the trailer, I _____ (wipe) the surface of every counter and cabinet; I also _____ (scrub) the floors.

l. When Ramon rented a big apartment, he _____ (suggest) I share it with him.

CHAPTER 19: USING VERBS CORRECTLY

Choosing the Correct Forms of be, have, *or* do *in Past and Present Tense*

Circle the correct form of the verb in each sentence below.

a. The supervisor of the night shift do/does several things to increase efficiency.

b. Unless the players compromise, the manager has/have to cancel the game.

c. United Vegetable Growers is/are a well-known company in this area.

d. Sammy and Arnold gave their mother a new car; they be/are devoted to their family.

e. I am using bleach on the bathroom tiles; I hope it do/does the job.

f. A week ago, Lucille and I was/were the best of friends.

g. When I was a child, my father have/had a long black beard.

h. My seven-year old son done/did his homework by himself every day for a month.

i. I know you didn't mean to hurt my feelings, but you was/were unkind yesterday.

j. Thanks to his meticulous planning and advertising, Paul have/had an enormous crowd for the restaurant's opening.

k. Last year, you was/were unhappy with your choice of college.

l. I refused to involve myself in the argument because it have/had nothing to do with me.

m. Whenever it snows, I be/am surprised by the beauty of nature.

n. My sister and I always cook a big dinner on Thanksgiving; we do/does it to give my mother a break.

o. Teresa and Anna rarely spend time together; clearly they are/be uncomfortable with each other.

CHAPTER 19: USING VERBS CORRECTLY

Correcting Errors in Verb Forms

Each sentence below contains one error in verb form. Cross out the incorrect form and write the correct form above the error.

a. The tour guide showed us the great hall of the castle and then lead us to the dungeon.

b. The gym teacher meant to be honest about the gymnast's progress, but the teacher shrunk from hurting the gymnast's feelings.

c. His brother has brought John nothing but trouble; I don't know how John has beared it for so long.

d. Last night, during the freeze, our pipes burst; it's the first time they have ever broke.

e. While the moviegoers stood in line for tickets, pickpockets creeped among the crowd.

f. Three times this week the family has woken in the night because somebody has rang the front doorbell.

g. That company is a reliable one; it has designed and builded some of the finest homes in the city.

h. When my boss payed me at the end of the week, I swore I would put that money in a savings account.

i. I feel sorry for Abdul, but he choosed to drop out of school, and so he brought his problems on herself.

j. I seen that the other students had finished the exam in only thirty minutes.

CHAPTER 19: USING VERBS CORRECTLY

Selecting the Correct Verb Form: A Comprehensive Exercise

In the blanks below, write the correct form of the verb indicated.

a. Every time I buy a lottery ticket, I _____ (be) optimistic about my chances.

b. That perfume _____ (smell) like roses and jasmine; it is lovely.

c. I know that man; he _____ (go) to my karate class every Thursday.

d. Samir had to have his car tuned: now it _____ (run) like a new car.

e. My brother _____ (realize) the truth when he read the letter from his best friend.

f. It's easy to make black beans and rice; I _____ (do) it all the time.

g. Ginger is a useful spice; it _____ (have) a distinctive flavour that is good with vegetables and chicken.

h. Kindergarten teaches my son to interact with other children; thus it _____ (be) a valuable program.

i. The bowling league from Pinehurst has _____ (beat) us for three years in a row.

j. When the wind grew stronger, the balloon _____ (blow) out of the child's hands.

k. My nephew screamed; another toddler had _____ (bite) his hand.

l. I will not buy that book; it _____ (cost) more than I can afford.

m. Last week I bought new tires; they _____ (cost) $50 more than my last set of tires.

n. Last night, Deon _____ (lie) on the most comfortable sofa to watch TV.

o. Deon has _____ (lie) on the most comfortable sofa every night for the past two months

p. We don't want to accept defeat because we _____ (fight) long and hard for that law.

q. After dark, the rat _____ (creep) out of the cellar and scurried up the stairs.

r. Just before we ate dinner, I _____ (lay) the bread and hummus on the table.

s. I had _____ (lay) the dishes on the table every night for dinner before my younger sister took over.

t. The coat was so old the elbows were _____ (wear) through, leaving big holes.

u. She is a good correspondent; she has _____ (write) to me every week.

CHAPTER 20: MORE ON VERBS: CONSISTENCY AND VOICE

Correcting Sentences That Are Inconsistent in Tense

In each sentence below, one verb is inconsistent in tense. Cross it out and write the correct tense above.

a.   On Saturdays I pick up the dry cleaning, shopped for groceries, stop at the drug store, and fill the car with gas.

b.   Last night a salesman called and offer us a cheaper rate on long distance calls, but the deal sounded fishy.

c.   My girlfriend gives me many compliments, and I appreciate them because I know she meant what she says.

d.   I spent hours selecting a gift and finding the right card; then I plan a special dinner and invited all his friends.

e.   I run and work out at a gym every day, so I keep my weight down and released stress.

f.   Since the restaurant is very popular, people arrived early and line up for a table.

g.   My dad was doing all the housework and taking care of the yard while my mom was cooking all the meals and paid the bills.

h.   As soon as I get home, I kick off my shoes and flopped into a comfortable chair.

i.   I love Sundays because I enjoy reading the Sunday papers, I cherished my first, leisurely cup of coffee, and I savour the time to unwind.

j.   We visited Niagara-on-the-Lake last fall; we walked down streets full of Victorian homes, shop in antique stores, and explored the marina.

CHAPTER 20: MORE ON VERBS: CONSISTENCY AND VOICE

Distinguishing Between the Past and the Present Perfect Tense

Circle the correct verb tense in each of the sentences below. Be sure to look carefully at the meaning of each sentence.

a.   Maurice called/has called me from his office last week.

b.   She volunteered/has volunteered at the children's festival for five years now.

c.   When Adam was at summer camp, he learned/has learned to swim.

d.   The Girl Guides were/have been selling cookies for many years.

e.   The doctor prescribed/has prescribed an antibiotic to fight the infection and advised the patient to get some rest.

f.   For years, I smoked/have smoked cigarettes; then I got smart and kicked the habit.

g.   Three of my friends were/have been crusading against smoking for many years now.

h.   Trevor climbed/has climbed a mountain in Tibet last fall.

i.   The gym was/has been running a special on new memberships, so I need to sign up soon.

j.   He was/has been a firefighter for ten years but quit to go to college.

k.   Nkele followed/has followed me home last night because my car sounded funny and he wanted to be sure I got home safely.

l.   Simon was/has been trying to get me to go to that movie for weeks now.

CHAPTER 20: MORE ON VERBS: CONSISTENCY AND VOICE

Distinguishing Between the Past and the Past Perfect Tense

Circle the correct verb tense in the sentences below. Be sure to look carefully at the meaning of each sentence.

a. Radeesh worked/had worked in a restaurant for ten years when he changed to a better job in a hotel.

b. The puppies trashed/had trashed the bedroom by the time I found them.

c. I raced to class, but the teacher gave/had given the quiz minutes earlier.

d. As she mixed the batter for the cake, she studied/had studied the recipe.

e. Every Friday, I grabbed my paycheque and ran/had run to the bank.

f. John was positive his brother stole/had stolen the petty cash earlier that afternoon.

g. When the judge announced the winner, the audience applauded/had applauded enthusiastically.

h. I was wondering if Freshteh called/had called the pizza place yet.

i. Inna fired questions at me while Jila teased/had teased me about my new haircut.

j. The soup simmered/had simmered for two hours before I added the final ingredient.

k. When I got to the play, I realized that Michael and his friends took/had taken the best seats in the theatre, so I sat at the back.

l. Every month, I wrote/had written a long letter to my family in China.

CHAPTER 20: MORE ON VERBS: CONSISTENCY AND VOICE

Rewriting Sentences to Correct Shifts in Voice

Rewrite the sentences below so that all the verbs are in the active voice. You may change the words to make the sentences clear, smooth, and consistent in voice.

a. Elaine was elected president yesterday; the club members voted at noon.

   rewritten: _____

   _____

b. The cheaper car should be chosen by you because it will not break your budget or cost a fortune in car insurance.

   rewritten: _____

   _____

c. A decision to close the restaurant was reached last week after the owners met with the bank representatives and discussed their finances.

   rewritten: _____

   _____

d. My neighbour was angry and hurt when he saw the damage that had been done to his garden by vandals.

   rewritten: _____

   _____

e. If a plan can be formed by the Crime Stoppers committee, Officer Woods will review it.

   rewritten: _____

   _____

f. I never understood the dangers of drunk driving until a high school classmate was hit by a drunk driver; my classmate suffered severe injuries.

   rewritten: _____

   _____

g. Hockey fans can be fanatics; every game is watched with intense concentration.

   rewritten: _____

   _____

h. The brainstorming of the paper was done by a group, but each student wrote his or her own draft and submitted it for peer review.

   rewritten: _____

   _____

i. Several solutions to the problem of school overcrowding were proposed by the school committee, yet they couldn't agree on one answer.

   rewritten: _____

   _____

CHAPTER 20: MORE ON VERBS: CONSISTENCY AND VOICE

Consistency and Voice: A Comprehensive Exercise

Most—but not all—of the sentences below have some kind of problem with verbs. The tense or voice may not be consistent, or there may be other errors in spelling or tense. Cross out the incorrect part of the sentence and write the correction above.

a. When Jacob visits his parents, he reminisces about the neighbourhood, filled them in on his latest adventures, and amuses them with funny stories.

b. Tina danced with the Royal Winnipeg Ballet for several years now.

c. Steve had called the pediatrician twice by the time the doctor returned the call.

d. When the baby was learning to walk, he grabbed every item in his path.

e. In a panic about missing the exam, Cody called the teacher's office and pleaded for a make-up test, but the teacher isn't willing to make an exception for Cody.

f. A few of the volunteers were paramedics for ten years now.

g. Even if you would have worked harder, you couldn't have met that deadline.

h. She already completed the puzzle when her mother said it was time for bed.

i. Dawn has finished her classes at the University of British Columbia last month.

j. Cara bought the invitations, I addressed them, and they were mailed by Charlie.

k. Whenever I see a movie about lawyers, I wish I would have gone to law school.

l. My mother told my brother he should of been more careful with my father's van; repairing the damage to the van would be expensive.

m. The runners were the best in the country because they maintained a strict exercise schedule and adhere to a healthy diet.

n. During his years as a truck driver, he learned to drive safely in all kinds of weather.

o.	A compromise was finally reached by the feuding neighbours after they bickered and complained.

p.	I will miss that restaurant because I use to meet my friends there, every Friday after work.

q.	The clean-up crew removed dead trees and bushes, bagged the broken bottles and discarded newspapers, and an old mattress was hauled away by the crew, also.

r.	The locksmith took a bus to work yesterday because he lost the keys to his car last week.

s.	If the police would have been five minutes earlier, they could have caught the robbers.

t.	He already replaced the broken glass in the window pane by the time she arrived at the store.

CHAPTER 21: MAKING SUBJECTS AND VERBS AGREE

Making Subjects and Verbs Agree: A Comprehensive Exercise

Circle the correct verb form in the sentences below.

a. Northern Steel, the new company in town, has/have a good record for maintaining an environmentally clean work site.

b. Everything in the boxes has/have been sorted and packed carefully.

c. The senior class at Carmichael High School is/are having a winter carnival next weekend.

d. Here is/are a copy of your birth certificate and your social insurance card.

e. Has/have anybody called the house lately?

f. Either of the books is/are suited for elementary school readers who like adventure stories.

g. I am positive that somebody is/are dumping garbage in the empty lot near my house.

h. Neither the plumbers nor the electrician has/have been paid for working on the office renovations.

i. One of that comedian's best movies is/are available on Blu-Ray.

j. Around the corner from the two gas stations is/are a tire store.

k. A representative of the United Students Councils is/are attending the seminar.

l. Under the tree grow/grows a fortune in truffles.

m. Among his greatest triumphs was/were the discovery of a new antibiotic.

n. At one time or another, everyone feel/feels lonely and bored.

o. Either my father or my aunts visit/visits my grandmother every day.

p. In the back of my closet is/are my old school uniform and an old blue teddy bear.

q. Not only the pre-school children but also their teacher has/have a love of outdoor games.

r. Breakfast and lunch is/are served on the hotel's patio.

s. There is/are a man in a baseball uniform and a small boy holding a baseball bat.

t. The clearest explanation of the issues is/are found in today's newspaper.

CHAPTER 22: USING PRONOUNS CORRECTLY: AGREEMENT AND REFERENCE

Making Pronouns and Antecedents Agree

For each sentence below, write the correct pronoun in the blank space.

a. The government of that country established _____ policies on immigration many years ago.

b. Everyone who joined the Boys' Athletic League brought _____ special talents to the group.

c. Mark looks forward to playing soccer on the weekends; _____ gives him a change to unwind.

d. Two of the actors who play detectives on the television show donated _____ time to the fundraiser.

e. One of the men in the audience cheered and threw _____ cap in the air.

f. I am sure everyone in the club did _____ best to make orientation week a success.

g. Someone from the Girl Guide troop must have lost _____ badge; I found it on the floor after the troop meeting.

h. Either of the puppies will make a great pet, especially if you are willing to spend time training _____.

i. I appealed to the committee because I believed _____ had been too harsh.

j. Each of the women contributed _____ own stories of success to the career workshop.

k. Visitors who get lost on the way to the monument can always consult _____ maps.

l. A ballerina in one of the most famous dance companies in the world has to practise constantly to maintain _____ position.

m. Some of the smartest people in the world have not learned to use _____ intelligence wisely.

n. Last week, a few friends dropped by; _____ stayed all afternoon and then took me out to dinner.

o. I wonder if anyone in the boys' choir practises _____ solo in the shower.

p. Carson Motors began a new advertising campaign; _____ wanted to appeal to older drivers.

q. Both of the houses needed repair and renovation; _____ particularly needed a coat of paint.

r. Neither of the sisters remembered where _____ had been at the time of the accident.

s. The coach was worried that the team would lose _____ standing in the association.

t. I want to thank everybody in the Club for _____ help.

CHAPTER 22: USING PRONOUNS CORRECTLY: AGREEMENT AND REFERENCE

Rewriting Sentences for Clear References of Pronouns

Rewrite the following sentences so that the pronouns have clear references. You can add, take out, or change words.

a. Pierre warned his father about his bad temper.

   rewritten: _____

   _____

b. My little brother doesn't mind going to the pediatrician because they always give him a cookie.

   rewritten: _____

   _____

c. She gave me a gift for my birthday which surprised me.

   rewritten: _____

   _____

d. Because Michelle likes biology, that is what she wants to be.

   rewritten: _____

   _____

e. When I went to pick up my jacket, they told me it hadn't been dry-cleaned yet.

   rewritten: _____

   _____

f. Last week I wrote a five-page essay which my instructor liked.

   rewritten: _____

   _____

g. Sunny Airlines provided a great benefits package, including a profit-sharing component, for their employees.

   rewritten: _____

   _____

h. When you close up, be sure to put everything back in their place.

   rewritten: _____

   _____

i. Raymond's mother is an engineer, so that's why he wants to study it.

   rewritten: _____

   _____

j. Each of the brothers spent the summer vacation working to pay for tuition at the college of their choice.

   rewritten: _____

   _____

CHAPTER 23: USING PRONOUNS CORRECTLY: CONSISTENCY AND CASE

Consistency in Pronouns

Circle any inconsistency in point of view in the sentences below. Cross out the incorrect pronoun(s) and write the correction above it.

a. Vacations can be a stressful time for me because I try to plan a vacation so special you'll remember it forever.

b. The staff isn't very friendly to you when my husband and I question the cable company about problems with our cable service.

c. My first year working at the store taught me that supervisors will be fair with me if you give them an honest day's work.

d. The children pushed against the fence, eager to see the arrival of the purple dinosaur and the treats he'd give you.

e. Swimmers have to be particularly careful of a riptide; it can carry you out to sea.

f. Ziad and Danica were confused by his speech; he spoke so softly you could hardly hear him.

g. When I arrived late for the movie, the theatre was so crowded you couldn't find a seat anywhere.

h. You never know what treasure I'll discover when I rummage through the merchandise at the thrift shop.

i. People always find comfort in remembering your happy times with loved ones.

j. Drivers have to be careful on mountain roads; if you aren't watching closely, you can drive right off the edge.

CHAPTER 23: USING PRONOUNS CORRECTLY: CONSISTENCY AND CASE

Choosing the Right Case of Pronoun

Circle the correct pronoun in each of the following sentences.

a. That town has lost much of its/it's charm for me.

b. I was sure the speaker's elaborate story was designed to make people like me/myself feel guilty.

c. Between you and I/me, I think he's more involved with Teresa than he says.

d. Lamarr and I/me took a trip to Brandon last week.

e. Him/He and his brother have never been able to find good jobs in the city.

f. Tom had nothing to do on Saturday, so I asked him to go with Bill and I/me.

g. It cost Melissa and I/me twenty dollars to take a cab to the restaurant.

h. My cousin had a house by the lake; when she died, she left the house to my brother and I/me.

i. We/Us and the plumber jumped when the water suddenly burst out of the faucet.

j. A panel of artists nominated two professional artists and me/myself for first prize in the poster contest.

k. Since the gift arrived with no card, my mother assumed it was from Reynaldo and I/me.

l. My family and I/myself are proud and happy to accept this award.

CHAPTER 23: USING PRONOUNS CORRECTLY: CONSISTENCY AND CASE

Consistency of Pronouns and Their Case: A Comprehensive Exercise

Circle the correct pronoun in the sentences below.

a. If the weather forecaster predicts a sunny day, you/I know I'd better bring an umbrella with me.

b. No one had considered the impact of the decision on my brother and me/myself.

c. The company must comply with safety regulations or it will lose its/it's license.

d. I may be taller than my sister, but she is more patient than I/me.

e. Me/I and Jason reviewed the history chapters all day.

f. I really want to surprise my wife, so we'll keep the party a secret between you and I/me.

g. He/Him and I/me have been friends for a long time.

h. I wish he wouldn't depend on you and I/me for entertainment.

i. Callers who get voice mail instead of a human being can become irritated; you/they become impatient pushing buttons.

j. The woman from the library and she/her carpool to work.

k. It was so hot that I turned on the air conditioner in my apartment; I/you couldn't survive without some cool air.

l. When a boy wanted to leave the classroom, you/he needed permission.

m. My advisors and I/myself have decided not to accept management's contract.

n. If you can't figure out how to assemble the bike, you can give it to he/him and I/me.

o. We/Us and Diane cleaned my grandmother's yard and cut the lawn.

CHAPTER 24: PUNCTUATION

Punctuating with Periods, Question Marks, and Semicolons

Add any necessary periods, question marks, and semicolons to the following sentences. Do not change or take out any existing punctuation marks. Do no change small letters to capital letters. Some sentences do not need any additional punctuation.

a.   He asked whether I wanted to go to the movies on Saturday

b.   James questioned Mrs Mehta about the missing documents.

c.   Will he ever stop borrowing money from his sister

d.   I wonder if there will ever be an end to the conflict

e.   Bill loved spicy food however, it aggravated his stomach problem.

f.   Bill loved spicy food, but it aggravated his stomach problem.

g.   You were wonderful in the play you kept the audience amused and entertained.

h.   Do you think she is sincere

i.   Jessica took good notes in class and reviewed them carefully before the exam.

j.   Jessica took good notes in class she reviewed them carefully before the exam.

k.   Jessica took good notes in class, and she reviewed them carefully before the exam.

l.   I would never change doctors I trust Dr. Spinelli.

m.   I am not sure whether to go to college near my home

n.   When are you going to make a decision about the wedding

o.   Suzanne can fix the sink she's a good plumber.

CHAPTER 24: PUNCTUATION

Punctuating with Commas

Put commas wherever they are needed in the following sentences. Do not add any other punctuation, and do not change any existing punctuation. Just add the necessary commas. Some of the sentences do not need commas.

a. Rain or shine we'll be there for the game on Saturday.

b. I was shocked to see I owed $2147 on my credit card.

c. The dog running across the street was my neighbour's lost pet.

d. Artichokes my husband's favourite vegetable are easy to cook.

e. Whenever you decide to go go prepared for any kind of weather.

f. Camera World which opened last month is the best place for bargains on film and lenses.

g. I get the freshest fruits and vegetables at the farmers' market the organic food store or the neighbourhood produce stand.

h. The car that I had dreamed of was parked in front of my apartment.

i. Jane once said "I'm not a selfish person."

j. You can run from the law but you can't hide forever.

k. Jimmy always bought expensive clothes but never looked good in them.

l. Sure I'll be happy to give Daniel a lift home.

m. August 29 1996 is the day we got married.

n. When the phone rang I raced to answer it.

o. Tim became very angry at the rude interruption yet he managed to control his temper.

CHAPTER 24: PUNCTUATION

Punctuating with Apostrophes

Add apostrophes where they are needed in the following sentences. Some sentences do not need apostrophes.

a. Ask Maria if shell pack Davids toys in a couple of sturdy cartons.

b. Its important to return that shirt with its sales receipt if you want your money back.

c. When I saw a sweater left behind at the movies, I didnt pick it up because I wasnt sure it was yours.

d. My grandson was invited to a childrens festival at his elementary school.

e. The neighbours rushed to our house to see the puppy we had found; they were sure it was theirs.

f. Jill asked Jack if hed take her to Jim and Lisas party.

g. That century-old house was beautiful; its a shame its front door couldnt be salvaged.

h. Cant you find some way to discover Phyllis favourite restaurant?

i. You should see the new movie about extraterrestrials; youll love the special effects.

j. All the gardening tools at the garage sale were theirs.

k. After I cleaned and polished the brass bowl, it regained its old lustre.

l. My brothers are sure the packages couldve been delivered to Mrs. Willis house instead of to their apartment.

m. Somebodys car keys have fallen behind the dresser; I hope theyre not yours.

n. If you get lost in the suburbs, theres an easy way to find your way back to my place.

o. I hope the jacket fits because shes spent hours altering the seams and shoulders.

CHAPTER 24: PUNCTUATION

Punctuating with Colons, Exclamation Marks, Dashes, Parentheses, and Hyphens

In the sentences below, add colons, exclamation marks, dashes, parentheses, or hyphens as needed. Answers may vary since some writers will use dashes instead of parentheses.

a. Every time he goes to the bakery, he brings home a variety of goodies cinnamon buns, pumpernickel bagels, and jelly doughnuts.

b. The woman who sang opera the last of the contestants was the best.

c. You're the father of a baby girl

d. Before I went away to summer camp, my mother told me three things eat your vegetables, write home, and wear clean underwear.

e. The meeting begins at seven and you'd better be on time.

f. Fieldbrook Airport the airport closest to my house is two hours away.

g. I see it now; you're an alien invader.

h. The table was beautifully set china plates shone, glasses sparkled, and coloured napkins glowed.

i. If you're going camping this weekend, take a warm jacket, a hat, and a heavy sleeping bag the temperature will be freezing.

j. Ellen had some half baked idea about finishing college in three years.

k. My cousin Elmo the little snitch told my mother I'd been stealing the cookies.

l. My father wanted a state of the art computer for his fiftieth birthday.

CHAPTER 24: PUNCTUATION

Punctuating with Quotation Marks, Underlining, and Capital Letters

In the sentences below, add any quotation marks, underlining, or capital letters as needed.

a. I'd like to meet him, Eddie said, but I'm all booked up next week.

b. I have no idea what dad wants for his birthday.

c. Sammy asked, Can I borrow your book?

d. If you want a shortcut to the auditorium, take the harbourview expressway to intercity mall.

e. Trina complained, you never clean up the kitchen. You leave the dirty dishes for me to do.

f. He asked if I had ever seen an old movie called Rocky, about a fighter.

g. You need to study more, his teacher said.

h. The only cereal my four-year-old will eat is kellogg's raisin bran.

i. My father loves the song called the long and winding road.

j. My husband will perform at Riverdale music hall in the spring.

k. I chose margaret atwood's poem entitled You Fit Into Me in a collection called power politics.

CHAPTER 24: PUNCTUATION

Punctuation: A Comprehensive Exercise

Add all the necessary punctuation to the following sentences.

a. Sylvia was sure she had lost the childrens winter hats but she kept looking in the garage and attic.

b. Writing the paper took me hours consequently I had no time to study for the quiz in my introduction to sociology class.

c. Carmen's Café which is the best pizza place in town is expanding its dining area.

d. If you need a ride to school she whispered you can ride with me.

e. I want to buy an air conditioner because I cant stand hot summer days humid summer nights and constant summer hayfever.

f. I wrecked my car and wound up with a bill for two thousand and forty-two dollars.

g. We used to sing O Canada at our meetings.

h. I need to buy some items for our medicine cabinet aspirin bandages cough medicine and antacid.

i. Lucy can watch the playoffs at my house or she can watch them on her own television.

j. David left Brampton Ontario on April 23 1981 and settled in Medicine Hat Alberta.

k. The driver who hit my car was not paying attention.

l. Your brother good or bad is still a member of your family.

m. I know father that youd rather be at Thomas house.

n. When he visited Sarajevo he saw the way children survive in a war torn country.

o. Nancy asked Are there any volunteers

p. Before I attended Middlebrook high school I had never been to a high school that offered courses like music appreciation and french literature.

q. Susan is taking the summer off then she'll start college at a school on the east coast.

r. For ten years, springfield chevrolet has been known for its fair deals and low prices consequently the company has grown and prospered.

s. Smooth talk my favourite movie is based on a short story called Where are you going? Where have you been? by Joyce Carol Oates.

APPENDIX: GRAMMAR FOR ESL STUDENTS

Identifying and Correcting Present Tense Verbs

Underline 13 present tense verbs in this paragraph. Then correct any verb errors in the space above the error. The first one is done for you. *Hint:* There are 5 present tense verb errors.

The plot of the movie *Titanic* <u>is</u> a tragic love story. Rose and Cal plans to get married. However, Rose falls in love with Jack Dawson on the Titanic. He stops her before she jumps over the railing. They dances at the party in steerage. Later she save him by cutting off his handcuffs. Before the ship sinks, Rose and Jack help many people to climb to the decks. She refuse to enter the lifeboat with the other rich people. The two lovers jumps into the water together; only Jack dies in the cold, cold sea. Despite its sad ending, the *Titanic* is one of my favourite movies.

APPENDIX: GRAMMAR FOR ESL STUDENTS

Revising Verb Tenses 1

Change the 13 verbs in this paragraph to the simple present tense. Write your correction in the space provided above each line. The first one is done for you:

is

Another one of my favourite movies ~~will be~~ *Anna and the King*. At the beginning of the film, Anna will travel to Burma to teach the King's children. She is going to teach them English, science, and modern ways. Her son Louis will come with her too. First, he will fight with the Crown Prince, and then they will become close friends. After awhile, Anna is hoping to change the King's ways. During her stay, she will understand many of the old Siamese traditions; Siam will also learn many things about the British way of life. For their part, the King and his prime minister will appreciate her democratic ideas. However, Anna will not be able to help Lady Tuptim or her lover Batel. Overall, there will be many changes in both Anna's and the King's lives.

APPENDIX: GRAMMAR FOR ESL STUDENTS

Revising Verb Tenses 2

Change the 16 verbs in this paragraph from present tense to simple past tense. Write your correction in the space provided above each line. The first one is done for you:

were
Fables ~~are~~ old, old stories. Each fable teaches a lesson or moral. Usually, the characters in the fable are animals that act like people. They talk and act silly; they are also clever sometimes.

In the fable "The Farmer and the Stork," the farmer thinks that the stork eats his corn. He then punishes not only the stork, but all the other birds as well. The farmer says that all the birds are guilty. The moral of the fable is "Birds of a feather flock together." Indeed, people still judge us by our friends and our family, not by who we are as individuals.

APPENDIX: GRAMMAR FOR ESL STUDENTS

Revising Contractions

Change the 13 contracted verb forms in this paragraph to their long form. Write your correction in the space provided above each line. The first one is done for you:

> ***would not***
> If people ~~wouldn't~~ be so impatient, driving would be less of an ordeal. If, for
> instance, the driver behind me didn't honk his horn as soon as the light's turned green,
> both he and I'd probably have lower blood pressure. He wouldn't be irritating himself by
> pushing so hard. And I wouldn't be reacting by slowing down, trying to irritate him even
> more. When I get impatient in traffic, I'm just making a bad situation worse. My hurry
> doesn't get me to my destination any faster; it just stresses me out.
>
> The impatient driver doesn't get anywhere; neither does the impatient customer at
> a restaurant. Impatience at restaurants doesn't pay. I've worked as a hostess at a
> restaurant, and I know that the customer who moans and complains about waiting for a
> table won't get one any faster than the person who makes the best of the wait. In fact, the
> customer who's too aggressive or obnoxious is likely to get slower service from the
> restaurant staff.

APPENDIX: GRAMMAR FOR ESL STUDENTS

Identifying and Correcting Articles

Correct the errors with *a, an,* or *the* in the following paragraph. You may need to add, change, or eliminate articles. Write the correction in the space provided above each line. There are 10 errors.

Students face all kinds of problems when they start the college. Some students struggle with lack of basic math skills; others have never learned to write term paper. Students who were stars in the high school have to cope with being just another student number at a large post-secondary institution. Students with the small children have to find a way to be the good parents and the good students too. Although many of problems are common, I found a even more typical conflict. Biggest problem in college was learning to organize my time.

Answer Key

Exercises for Writing in Steps:

The Process Approach

Some of the exercises do not have specific answers. Instead, they ask students to do such things as brainstorm, write descriptions, or add detail. These activities have no answers in the key. Other exercises have a variety of answers, and a possible response is provided.

CHAPTER 1: WRITING A PARAGRAPH

page 5   *Finding Specific Details in Freewriting*

Answers will vary. Possible answers include

Doing errands: Never seem to have enough time. Always seem to be racing around. Shopping at supermarket. I like to buy goodies. Never buy food when you're hungry. Do errands on lunch hour. Get frustrated by lack of time.

Vacations: Family vacations. When I was a kid, we went to the beach every summer. Lots of new water toys. Different attitudes towards sun exposure.

page 6   *Writing Topic Sentences for Lists of Details*

Answers will vary. Possible responses include

a. Contact with nature brings us many benefits.
b. Although I use my laptop all the time, sometimes I wonder why I bring it to school.
c. People marry for a number of reasons.

page 8   *Revising a Rough Lines Draft by Combining Sentences*

My little sister has too many toys. <u>Megan has six huge stuffed animals covering her bed.</u> She has a variety of dolls. <u>She got Hanna Montana from my aunt, two dolls that look like characters from</u> *High School Musical* <u>from my cousin, and a Cinderella doll from my mother.</u> If she gets tired of dolls, Megan has other toys. She has a toy kitchen with a plastic table, stove, and refrigerator. She has an elegant doll's house, too. Megan has toys for every occasion and location. <u>She owns beach, bath, car, and bedtime toys.</u> She has so many toys, she has nowhere to put them. <u>They are scattered all over the house, so I can't help tripping over them.</u>

Some people think that all Italian food is bad for you, but they are mistaken. For one thing, studies have <u>proven</u> that olive oil, which is a common ingredient in Italian food, can be good for you. It can have a healthy <u>effect</u> on <u>cholesterol</u> levels. And while many people think Italian food is fattening, it <u>doesn't</u> have to be. There are many things on an Italian menu, like fresh <u>fruits</u> and <u>vegetables</u>, chicken, and fish. Many people think all pasta is fattening, but pasta doesn't have to be <u>fattening; it's</u> [or <u>fattening. It's</u>] what you put on it that counts. A delicious sauce made from fresh tomatoes, garlic, and herbs can be healthy and low in calories. Italian cooking has so much <u>variety; it</u> [or <u>variety. It</u>] has something for every kind of eater from the <u>health-conscious</u> to the <u>dieter</u>.

CHAPTER 2: WRITING FROM READING

page 10   ***Paraphrasing***

Answers will vary.

page 10   ***Correcting the Errors in a Final Lines Reaction to Reading***

Looking for a close parking spot is silly, Gwinn Owens says, and I agree with him. My mother spends twenty minutes driving around a parking lot, looking for a good <u>space. In</u> that time she could have <u>gone</u> into the store and finished her shopping. My <u>sister is</u> so crazy she parks in a fire lane to go the <u>ATM,</u> and she has been ticketed twice. I am <u>smarter; I</u> [or <u>smarter. I</u>] <u>just</u> take the first spot I can find, close or not. I walk the extra few <u>steps</u> to the store or movies or bank. <u>Then I'm</u> on my way while other people are still circling the parking lot, looking for a good space.

CHAPTER 3: ILLUSTRATION

page 11   ***Eliminating Details That Don't Fit***

a. Bosses get paid more than most workers. Bosses should not be allowed to leave early if workers can't.
b. Subways are efficient means of transportation. I would never do my banking online.
c. Gingerbread houses are tedious to make. Many children associate Easter with the Easter bunny.

page 12   ***Revising Long Sentences***

1. According to this business article, the 3-D theatre has been losing profits for years. As well, attempts to make Hollywood action movies in 3-D have not increased customer demand.
2. In this computer age, people are reluctant to purchase hard copies of encyclopaedias. Instead, they prefer to get free online information or to use Microsoft's best-selling Encarta software.
3. As a result of the bird flu scare, supermarkets and fast-food chains have experienced a sales slump and face potential layoffs. In addition, millions of small farmers are losing a valuable source of income as their poultry is slaughtered.

4. The Baby Boomers are investing in larger homes, rather than retiring to small units. While retailers profit from more furniture sales to these Boomers, their children will likely receive a reduced inheritance.

CHAPTER 4: DESCRIPTION

page 13   ***Identifying Sentences That Are Too General***

      a. 1   b. 2   c. 3   d. 2   e. 3

page 15   ***Putting Details in Order***

      a. 4,5,1,2,3   b. 2,1,5,3,4

page 17   ***Correcting Errors in Final Lines***

My bicycle ride through Tudor Woods was an escape into a natural haven. The narrow country roads <u>were</u> fringed by tall pine trees, and the trees created a dark, dense <u>environment</u>. <u>Riding</u> under the canopy of trees, I smelled the green smell of pine <u>needles; I</u> [or <u>needles. I</u>] felt the crunch of pine cones under the bike's wheels. No one <u>was</u> there <u>except</u> me and the creatures of the woods. The <u>squirrels</u> were <u>not</u> afraid of me. They just <u>stopped</u> and stared at me as I rode by. Several blue jays dipped and swooped close to my face. Maybe they were <u>curious</u>. In one place, I saw <u>an</u> owl sitting high in a <u>tree. He</u> [or <u>tree; he</u>] seemed mysterious and calm. The woods were a tranquil and beautiful retreat for me. They <u>showed</u> me a different world from my <u>busy</u> city life.

CHAPTER 5: NARRATION

page 18   ***Writing the Missing Topic Sentences in Narrative Paragraphs***

Answers will vary. Possible responses include

a. Selling lemonade was an enjoyable way for Suzanne and Katie to become part of the community.
b. A bad experience at work led me to discover my dog's capacity for sympathy.
c. I saw another side of Cameron at a talent contest.

page 20   ***Distinguishing Good Topic Sentences from Bad Ones in Narration***

a. X	f. X	k. X
b. X	g.	l.
c.	h.	m.
d. X	i. X	n.
e.	j.	o. X

page 21   ***Developing a Topic Sentence from a List of Details***

Answers will vary. Possible topic sentences include

a. After I joined a gossip session, I felt like a coward.
b. Ever since my neighbour's apartment was robbed, I am more careful about my safety.

a. 7, 1, 5, 3, 2, 4, 6
b. 9, 1, 2, 3, 4, 7, 5, 6, 8

A visit to my father's workplace helped me understand him. <u>Before</u> my visit, I considered my father an irritable man. <u>Every night</u> he would come home snarling and snapping. <u>Then</u> I saw where and how he worked. <u>The first thing</u> I noticed about his workplace was the noise. Several people talked at once, and they all spoke loudly. <u>Meanwhile</u>, phones were ringing. <u>As soon as</u> my father walked in, someone shouted, "Jim! Over here! We need you!" He rushed to help. <u>Next</u>, a different person called, "Jim! Come on! I need you to show me how to work this machine." <u>At the same time</u>, my father picked up a ringing telephone. "Let me put you on hold for one second," he said. The pressure and pace continued until closing time. <u>Finally</u>, my exhausted father, the last to go home, packed up and left. I was exhausted just from watching him. <u>Now</u> I understand why he might come home tired and cranky.

I will never forget my first day at college. Although I hadn't <u>gotten</u> much sleep the night before, I still <u>woke before my alarm went</u> off in the morning. I <u>was</u> feeling very excited and anxious when I arrived at the college campus<u>;</u> there were so many people walking the halls. I soon got lost. However, student volunteers <u>were</u> wandering the <u>hallways </u>and one offered to help me. I <u>found</u> my class with a few minutes to spare. I felt even more nervous when I looked around the classroom and found that I was probably the oldest student there. Then the professor walked <u>in</u> and said<u>,</u> "<u>G</u>ood morning." The class did an introductory <u>exercise</u> and I <u>learned</u> the names of all my classmates<u>;</u> many were in the same program as <u>I</u>. I felt my nervousness ease. My other classes <u>were</u> similar and by the end of the day<u>,</u> I made some friends. I am now at the end of my first semester<u>,</u> and I am so happy I decided to come to college<u>.</u> I would recommend it to anyone.

CHAPTER 6: PROCESS

a. OK	e. OK	i. B
b. S	f. S	j. OK
c. B	g. OK	k. A
d. A	h. B	l. OK

a. 6, 2, 1, 3, 4, 5, 7
b. 4, 5, 1, 2, 3, 6
c. 1, 5, 2, 3, 4

Richard has a foolproof system for ironing his cotton dress shirts. First he makes sure the iron is on "Steam" and the steam section is filled with water. <u>Second</u> he carefully irons the collar, making sure no fabric wrinkles near the seams. <u>After he finishes the collar,</u> he fits each shoulder around the end of the ironing board and irons the shoulders and top of the sleeves. <u>Next</u> he irons the main part of the shirt, from shoulder to bottom edge, very slowly. <u>Afterward</u> he irons the part around the buttons. He is careful not to burn the buttons by ironing on top of them. <u>As soon as he has completed the button area,</u> he does the sleeves and <u>finally,</u> the cuffs. When he is finished, he has a professional-looking shirt.

page 28   *Correcting Errors in Final Lines*

Chris knows exactly how to get away with <u>being</u> late for math class. First of all, he <u>always looks</u> very apologetic when he comes in late. He <u>whispers,</u> <u>"Excuse me,"</u> and he slinks past the teacher. Then <u>Chris</u> creeps to the back of the room on tiptoe, and he silently <u>takes</u> a desk in the corner. All <u>through</u> class, he looks humble and distressed. At the end of class, he <u>waits until</u> all the other <u>students</u> <u>have</u> left the room. Finally, he approaches the teacher. His eyes <u>are</u> tearful as he apologizes for being late. It never <u>fails.</u> [or <u>fails;</u>] <u>Chris</u> always gets away with his rude behaviour.

CHAPTER 7: COMPARISON/CONTRAST

page 29   *Writing Appropriate Transitions for a Comparison or Contrast Paragraph*

Answers will vary. Possible responses include

- b. My sister has a talent for singing, but my mother is a gifted member of a community drama group.
- c. Going to the movies can cost as much as thirteen dollars a person; on the other hand, renting a video can cost five dollars for a whole family.
- d. Both keeping a journal and writing poetry are outlets for your emotions.
- e. Although my studio is an organized environment, my house is a chaotic place.
- f. My sister is a brilliant mathematician; however, I am lost when it comes to numbers.

page 30   *Finding Differences in Subjects That Look Similar*

Answers will vary. Possible responses include

- a. height of driver seat from the ground, maneuverability, stability in a high wind
- b. number of classes weekly, textbooks, amount of homework
- c. kinds of reading material, level of attentiveness, time spent reading without a break
- d. price, taste, texture
- e. ease of moving, degree of privacy, maintenance fees

page 31   *Writing Topic Sentences for Comparison or Contrast*

Answers will vary. Possible topic sentences include

- a. Writing a letter and making a phone call differ in their required time, necessary materials, and lasting impact.
- b. Writing a letter and making a phone call are both communication from a distance, for similar purposes, and at a similar cost.

page 32   *Correcting the Errors in Final Lines*

Unlike my first job, my current job is exhausting, demanding, and stressful. I got my first job informally, when I was twelve. My Aunt Raquel was moving out of her apartment, and she needed help with packing and loading boxes into a rented truck. She said she would [or she'd] pay me twenty dollars for helping her one Saturday. She worked beside me, and we took breaks whenever we felt tired. We played the radio and danced from box to box. All in all, it was an enjoyable way to earn twenty dollars. Today I work at a fast food restaurant where I am on my feet all day. I work eight-hour shifts and almost never have time to take a break. My manager is always checking up on me, insisting that I work faster. Sometimes he says I am not friendly enough to the customers. I am constantly nervous because I imagine the manager is standing behind me, waiting to criticize. At the end of my shift, I long for the time when I was a twelve-year-old moving person.

CHAPTER 8: CLASSIFICATION

page 33   ***Finding Categories That Fit One Basis for Classification***

Answers will vary. Possible responses include

b. 1. long marriages, 2. medium-length marriages, 3. short marriages
c. 1. computers used for record keeping, 2. computers used to send messages, 3. computers used to play games
d. 1. clothes for weddings, 2. clothes for funerals, 3. clothes for going out

page 34   ***Combining Sentences for a Better Classification Paragraph***

I can classify my books by their place in my room; there are books on the desk, books on the bookcase, and books on my night table. The books on my desk are my schoolbooks. They are the books I need to read as soon as I can. <u>They include my Algebra I, Introduction to Public Speaking, and Art Appreciation books.</u> These books are neatly stacked in a prominent place, but I tend to avoid them because they represent the hard work I have to do. The books in my bookcase are books I've acquired over the years. They are books I will read someday. <u>They include biographies and classics like *Two Solitudes*, which an English teacher recommended to me.</u> These books are stacked up, but there are so many books, the stacks are beginning to fall over. The last kind of book is the kind on my night table. I read one of these books every night. They are entertaining books like mysteries or thrillers. <u>They are tumbling all over the night table because I keep piling up new books I can't wait to read.</u> All my books serve some purpose in my life, but some volumes are more attractive than others.

page 35   ***Correcting Errors in Final Lines***

My experience as a coffee drinker has led me to believe that the coffee I drink can be classified according to the situation I'm in. There <u>is</u> the coffee I drink every morning on my way to work. Because I drink this coffee every day, I restrict myself to the cheap, sugar-filled caffeine fix that Canadians can <u>find</u> on every street corner. These morning coffees are quick, cheap, and give me the boost I need to get my morning started. It's not my favourite coffee, but it does the trick. By the late afternoon<u>,</u> my energy starts to lag<u>,</u> so it's time for another coffee<u>.</u> If I'm lucky enough to be near a café that sells iced coffee drinks<u>,</u> I'll get one. Even if it is winter<u>,</u> I will buy an iced coffee. The only problem is the price<u>;</u> with the price of an iced coffee<u>,</u> I could buy lunch instead. Finally there is the coffee I like to drink after dinner. After a fancy dinner<u>,</u> there's nothing like a latté after dessert. This latté might cost me double what one would cost in my local store<u>,</u> but <u>it's</u> worth it. When I think of all the <u>different</u> coffees I buy<u>,</u> I realize I could probably buy a small car<u>, but</u> I figure that I need a treat now and then.

CHAPTER 9: CAUSE AND EFFECT

page 36   ***Creating Causes or Effects for Topic Sentences***

Answers will vary. Acceptable suggestions include

b. 1. They are worried about their teen's safety; 2. they want to maintain some discipline at home; and 3. they suspect teens of alcohol or drug use.
c. 1. You have to report lost credit cards; 2. you have to replace your driver's license; and 3. you lose the money in your wallet.

d. 1. Children love the attention; 2. children learn to share quiet times with a parent; and 3. parents find fulfillment in a simple ritual.

e. 1. A student's printer might not be working; 2. a student may have been sick; and 3. a student may not have been able to find his/her professor.

page 37 *Making the Connections Clear*

Answers will vary. Possibilities include

a. Some insecure people feel that clothes with designer labels can give them status, so they buy designer clothes.

b. Matthew broke up with Brittany because she has a hard time showing the affection that he needs.

c. Although I'm on a budget, I love movies enough to want to spend my money on them. I save money and am able to enjoy movies by renting movies instead of going to the theatre.

d. I never did much reading in high school. Now that I am in college, which requires a great deal of difficult reading assignments, I am having a hard time keeping up with all the material.

page 38 *Recognizing Transitions in Cause or Effect*

I miss my old neighbourhood because it was familiar, friendly, and full of things to do. <u>First of all</u>, I grew up in that neighbourhood, and I knew every part of it. I could tell any stranger the location of the nearest convenience store or the closest pay phone. I knew which stores were running specials on soft drinks and which restaurants had the best fries. <u>Secondly</u>, my old neighbourhood was a friendly place. Everybody knew everybody else. On summer nights, people sat on their front stoops and talked to each other. My mother was always babysitting for the neighbour's children, or a neighbour was babysitting for us. People helped each other out. <u>And most important</u> to me, as a child, was all the activity in the neighbourhood. There was always somebody to play ball with or just to hang out with. An empty lot on the corner made a great playground, and the abandoned shell of a building made a great playhouse. <u>Because</u> there were so many children in the area, and such great spaces for hiding, plotting, fighting, and playing, every day was an adventure for me.

page 39 *Correcting Errors in Final Lines*

Taking a class in Mandarin had unexpected results. While I took the class because it was required for my International Business program, I was surprised to find out that I am very good at learning a foreign <u>language. I</u> [or <u>language; I</u>] had the highest grade on the final exam, and my quiz average was excellent<u>,</u> too. My success in <u>Mandarin has</u> convinced me to take another Chinese-language course. Another result of my taking the class is my increased interest in Chinese customs and culture. I have begun to pay more attention to the cultural events in my community. I recently saw my first kung-fu <u>movie; it</u> [or <u>movie. It</u>] was great. In the evenings, I find myself searching the Internet for Chinese tourist attractions. The most exciting effect of my becoming a Mandarin student is my planned vacation. This summer, I am taking a trip to Beijing. I hope my Mandarin lessons will help me on my Chinese <u>adventure.</u> I never thought a required class like Mandarin would introduce myself to a world of new people, places, and <u>ideas.</u>

CHAPTER 10: ARGUMENT

page 40   ***Recognizing Good Topic Sentences for an Argument Paragraph***

a.	d.	g.	j.	m. OK
b.	e.	h. OK	k.	n. OK
c. OK	f.	i.	l.	o.

page 41   ***Distinguishing Between Reasons and Details***

a. *reason*: The coaches in minor league hockey are often too demanding
   details: One coach in my neighbourhood ridicules players who don't perform well.
   reason: The parents who attend minor league games can be aggressive and cruel.
   details: One parent called a player an idiot.
       A parent attacked a referee about a bad call.
   reason: The pressure hurts the children who play.
   details: Some children burst into tears if they miss a shot.
       I have seen children who are trembling before a game.

b. *reason*: The college pub has a superficial purpose: to encourage students to socialize.
   details: My brother dropped out of college because the pressure to socialize and drink hurt his grades.
       The student union offers many other social activities for students, activities that do not involve drinking.
   reason: The temptation to party often becomes too strong for some students to resist.
   details:: Many students plan their week and visit the pub only on their nights off.
       Others, like a friend of mine, practically live in the pub.
   reason:: College is for studying, not partying.
   details: Students who want to drink and party can find alternate pubs off campus.

page 42   ***Working with the Order of Reasons in an Argument Outline***

a. 3   b. 3   c. 2   d. 1

page 43   ***Combining Sentences in a Argument Paragraph***

<u>Almost every time I am on the road, I see someone driving and using a phone at the same time.</u> I believe we must outlaw the use of a phone while a person is driving. The driver who is talking on a phone makes it harder for me to drive. I have seen those who are talking and driving slip into another lane and even weave all over the road. <u>When I am near such a driver, I have to watch out for erratic behaviour.</u> Since the driver on the phone is not paying attention, I have to pay extra attention. Phone drivers create problems for themselves. <u>They may be driving with one hand or be preoccupied by their conversations.</u> Either way, they are likely to run into a tree or a wall. Worst of all, phone drivers create safety problems for others. <u>Their carelessness can cause them to ignore a red light or a turn signal or to follow too closely.</u> They may not hurt themselves, but they may hurt others. I have nothing against phones in cars. I think they are wonderful safety devices—as long as drivers pull off the road to use them.

page 44   ***Correcting Errors in Final Lines***

My college <u>needs</u> a club <u>specifically</u> designed for older students. Students who are thirty or over come to school feeling very <u>anxious. They</u> [or <u>anxious; they</u>] are not sure they can do the work, and they think all the younger students are much smarter. Older students tend to <u>feel</u> lost and alone<u>;</u> a <u>club</u> would <u>welcome</u> them to college and put them at ease. In addition a club could help them with their special concerns. Students in their <u>thirties</u> and <u>forties</u> are different from students right out of high school. Many are <u>parents;</u> some are grandparents. They may be more concerned with a college day care centre than with college social activities. They may <u>want</u> more job placement seminars than basketball games. Finally, a club for older students would give them power. If older students work together, they can <u>achieve</u> much more <u>than</u> if they work alone. The club could campaign for campus child care facilities or better job placement. A club could be a way to make older students feel <u>as if</u> <u>they're</u> a real part of college life.

CHAPTER 11: WRITING AN ESSAY

page 45   ***Identifying the Main Points in the Draft of an Essay***

Thesis: Until I actually experienced an ice storm, I had no idea of the damage it could do.
Topic Sentence Paragraph 2:   Before the storm, I really didn't believe the warnings of the weather channel.
Topic Sentence Paragraph 3:   When the storm was over, I came out of the wreckage and faced the reality of a killer ice storm.
Topic Sentence for Conclusion: Because of the storm, I did gain one thing: a more realistic view of what an ice storm can do.

page 48   ***Correcting Errors in Final Lines***

Accident Prone [no quotation marks]

Some people get hurt in <u>terrible</u> accidents. They get hit by a car, or they fall from <u>great</u> heights. I, on the other hand, get hurt in silly, stupid accidents. I can find an accident in the safest places.

One safe place where <u>I</u> <u>managed</u> to have an accident was the beach. I was by myself, <u>taking</u> advantage of a beautiful day by walking along the edge of the water. Suddenly I found the only <u>hole</u> in a flat, smooth beach. My foot hit the hole. I tripped and <u>fell</u> headlong on the sand. My face hit the only pebble on the beach, and I <u>chipped</u> my front tooth. On a perfect, sunny day, when the water was as flat as glass, I <u>managed</u> to have a beach <u>accident</u> without even going into the water. Other people have boating injuries or beach volleyball injuries, but I had a beach *walking* injury.

My next injury <u>occurred</u> at another unusual place, my desk in Business Math class. I was getting <u>ready</u> to turn in my homework, and I <u>needed</u> to <u>staple</u> the two <u>sheets</u> of problems. I pulled my tiny stapler from my backpack and tried to staple the homework. But my stapler jammed. In a panic, I tried to break open the parts of the stapler. Pounding the stapler against the top of my desk, <u>I got</u> a pencil jammed into the stapler. All I got was a pencil with a broken point. In desperation, I stuck my finger into the jammed parts. The sections opened; then they snapped <u>closed</u> again—around my finger! I was ashamed to be the only student injured while turning in his or her math homework.

I know that insurance companies <u>sell</u> special insurance for people with hazardous jobs. I wonder if they sell insurance for people like me. I need a insurance policy that covers hazards in safe places. <u>They're</u> the places where accidents seem to find me.

Answer Key
Quizzes and Extra Exercises for the
Reading Selections

CHAPTER 3: ILLUSTRATION

page 51   *Quiz on "Sticky Stuff"*

1. they all help to attach or to glue things together temporarily
2. burrs
3. one side of the fastener has a velvety texture; the other side is rough and looped; the two textures come together as do the two words
4. diaper tabs, machine-gun mounts, clothing, and more
5. 3M
6. *similar*: both attach temporarily, are easy to remove
   different: adhesive tape repairs rips in paper, Post-It notes serve briefly as reminders
7. *fact*: the products help to attach and to repair objects in day-to-day use
   exaggeration: the products solve only small problems on a daily basis; they are handy but not essential

CHAPTER 4: DESCRIPTION

page 52   *Quiz on "A Present for Popo"*

1. grandmother
2. Answers will vary. Possibilities include the following: to take her heart medicine, where she put her handbag, she had talked to you moments before, how much money she had in her billfold, when the author was getting married.
3. several import/export shops, plastic lanterns
4. a loudspeaker playing top-40 hits
5. a terrarium, for good luck
6. naughty spirits
7. heart attack, 91
8. Answers will vary. Possibilities include the following: a marching band, a New Orleans-like procession, Popo's large picture on a flat-bed truck
9. 8
10. Popo's children would no longer speak to each other.

page 53   *Finding Sense Descriptions in "A Present for Popo"*

Answers will vary. Possible answers are

a. description: "a holiday feast of honey-baked ham and mashed potatoes"
   sense(s) appealed to: taste
b. description: "Her window had a view of several import-export shops below, not to mention the grotesque plastic hanging lanterns and that nasty loudspeaker serenading tourists with 18 hours of top-forty popular hits."
   sense(s) appealed to: sight, hearing

c. description: "the wrinkled faces of a half-dozen grannies would peek cautiously out their windows"
   sense(s) appealed to: sight
d. description: "Her neighbors would cluck and sigh"
   sense(s) appealed to: hearing
e. description: "They burned incense."
   sense(s) appealed to: smell

CHAPTER 5: NARRATION

page 55   ***Quiz on "One Caring Teacher Set Things Right"***

Answers will vary. Possible answers include:

1. He feels the "power of life and light" around him.
2. He was stereotyped in a "harder" world, "the idea of Indians . . . set in concrete."
3. It was assumed that he was "slow, a difficult learner, too quiet for a kid and lethargic."
4. Astigmatism prevented Wagamese from learning to write properly.
5. According to Wagamese, caring allows us to help other people.

page 55   ***Recognizing Specific Details in "Back to Normal"***

Answers will vary. Possible answers include

a. shape shifter; hardening; purple moving upward into pearl grey
b. mill town school; northern Ontario; different world
c. But in the beginning, learning to write was a test, a challenge, an ordeal.
d. Walking through those big glass doors was terrifying for me; Walking back to my seat that day I felt ashamed, stupid and terribly alone.
e. upside down and backwards

CHAPTER 6: PROCESS

page 56   ***Quiz on "How to Get a Reference Letter"***

Answers may vary. Possible responses include

1. Educational institutions require reference letters because these letters address a student's "ability, character and personality."
2. The sample letter is too meek, and the student tries to make his/her case too late.
3. The "three pillars" are course selection, choice of professors, and behaviour in class.
4. Potter recommends not asking non-tenured faculty for reference letters because such faculty often have "very little status within the profession," and are occasionally difficult to locate.
5. Other required items include a writing sample, statement of research interest, standardized test scores, and a transcript.
6. they know who you are; what you are like; how your mind works

CHAPTER 7: COMPARISON/CONTRAST

page 57   ***Quiz on "Hey, Canada's One Cool Country"***

Answers may vary. Possible responses include

1. point-by-point
2. Canadians are clean-cut, quiet, tidy, and polite
3. political policy (war in Iraq); policy on marijuana possession; gun control; same-sex marriages
4. order and good government
5. Canada is called progressive; Canadian society is "sound;" Canada is "cool."

CHAPTER 8: CLASSIFICATION

page 58   ***Quiz on "I'm a Banana and Proud of It"***

Answers may vary. Possible responses include

1. true
2. 'Banana' means "yellow on the outside and white inside."
3. According to Choy, "cultural history" made him a banana.
4. They still preferred to immigrate to Canada because they would likely starve in China.
5. The Second World War changed the discriminatory attitudes towards the Chinese because Chinese men "volunteered and lost their lives" as members of the military.
6. Nicknames replace formal names to keep a child humble.
7. They became distanced from their history.
8. Immigrants face the struggle between their cultural histories and being North American.
9. Being both Chinese and not Chinese
10. security and happiness

CHAPTER 9: CAUSE AND EFFECT

page 59   ***Quiz on "Saving the Planet One Swamp at a Time"***

1. Vancouver
2. The swamp made Suzuki, as a boy, realize how vast the world was and how 'puny' he was in comparison.
3. Warmer weather in Canada, "vineyards in Winnipeg, farms in the Arctic" might cause people not to be concerned with global warming
4. burning fossil fuels; deforestation
5. Responses may vary, and may include: "falling water tables, retreating lakeshores, acidification of oceans, shrinking ice caps and glaciers, expanded ranges for invasive species"
6. Smog is "created from a chemical reaction in the atmosphere between automobile and smokestack
7. increased infrastructure needs and healthcare costs

CHAPTER 10: ARGUMENT

page 60   **Quiz on "Have We Forgotten the Trojan Horse?"**

1. the fall of the Berlin Wall
2. We are a culture as much defined by what we buy as what we believe.
3. many fundamental human rights
4. If we protest and make a noise, things can happen.
5. the Third World (labour practices)
6. a satellite dish
7. television monitors in classrooms
8. two to 2 ½ minutes of commercials
9. lobbying [the governments] against funding cuts
10. risky to offend public opinion

page 61   **Quiz on "Assimilation, Pluralism, and 'Cultural Navigation': Multiculturalism in Canadian Schools"**

1. True
2. True
3. False; " . . . according to *assimilationists* . . ."
4. False; legally perhaps, in reality, no
5. False; means "leadership"
6. True
7. True
8. False; experience tells us otherwise
9. False; the author argues that ESL students are mainstreamed too soon
10. True

page 62   **Completing an Outline of "Assimilation, Pluralism, and 'Cultural Navigation': Multiculturalism in Canadian Schools""**

I. Thesis: The differences between the assimilation and pluralism approaches to Canada's multiculturalism will leave a mark on our future.
II. Many established and powerful educators in Canada choose the assimilation paradigm.
   A. Participation in Canadian public life should foster a sense of common heritage.
   B. *Canadian values should be given priority in the curriculum.*
   C. *All Canadian must separate their public and private cultural obligations.*
III. Assimilationists promote common Canadian values because they fear differences.
   A. *Focus on cultural diversity weakens Canada's fragile identity.*
   B. Exploring cultural ancestry will ghettoize students.
   C. *Competing cultural and religious groups will result in vendettas.*
IV. The assimilationists' alarm is based on three factors.
   A. *fear of change*
   B. *loss of cultural leadership*
   C. *naive understanding of culture*
V. Pluralist advocates promote the more global connections of Canadian students.
   A. *The cultural composition of Canada is no longer just European/American.*
   B. *Demographics reveal large Asian, African, South American, and Chinese populations.*
   C. Students need to learn how to interact with their multicultural peers in public space.
VI. Pluralists do not advocate an "either-or" scenario of cultural loyalties.
   A. *Our brains are cognitively equipped to deal with cultural diversity.*
   B. *Ancestral cultures and Canadian national heritage do not cancel each other out.*

VII. The consequences of not promoting the pluralist approach to multiculturalism are manifold.
  A. Students will seek other ways to reinforce their personal and cultural identity.
  B. *ESL students will continue to receive minimal language training.*
  C. *Canadian schools will become polarized between cultural groups and the mainstream.*
VIII. Conclusion: Canadian educators must foster the cultural intelligence of their students and adopt a pluralist pedagogy to prepare them for life.

CHAPTER 11: WRITING AN ESSAY

page 64 Quiz on "When Immigration Goes Awry"

1. False
2. True
3. True
4. False
5. False
6. True
7. False
8. False
9. True
10. True

page 65 Quiz on "Joined in Jihad?"

1. False; not *all* Muslims in *all* nations
2. True
3. True
4. False; the author argues that peace and prosperity reduce suspicions
5. True
6. False; means "in constant change"
7. True
8. False; the author himself hopes to bridge the gap somewhat
9. True
10. True

Answer Key
The Bottom Line: Grammar for Writers

page 68　　　*The Bottom Line: A Diagnostic Grammar Test*

Item Number　　*Section in Text and Grammar Concept*

a. 1　　　　Section 2: Coordination
b. 2　　　　Section 2: Coordination
c. 2　　　　Section 2: Coordination
d. 1　　　　Section 3: Subordination
e. 1　　　　Section 3: Subordination
f. 2　　　　Section 4: Avoiding Sentence Fragments
g. 2　　　　Section 4: Avoiding Sentence Fragments
h. 2　　　　Section 4: Avoiding Sentence Fragments
i. 1　　　　Section 5: Using Parallelism in Sentences
j. 1　　　　Section 5: Using Parallelism in Sentences
k. 2　　　　Section 6: Correcting Problems with Modifiers
l. 2　　　　Section 6: Correcting Problems with Modifiers
m. 2　　　Section 7: Using Verbs Correctly
n. 2　　　Section 7: Using Verbs Correctly
o. 1　　　　Section 8: More on Verbs: Consistency and Voice
p. 1　　　　Section 8: More on Verbs: Consistency and Voice
q. 1　　　　Section 9: Making Subjects and Verbs Agree
r. 2　　　　Section 9: Making Subjects and Verbs Agree
s. 1　　　　Section 10: Using Pronouns Correctly: Agreement and Reference
t. 1　　　　Section 10: Using Pronouns Correctly: Agreement and Reference
u. 2　　　　Section 11: Using Pronouns Correctly: Consistency and Case
v. 2　　　　Section 11: Using Pronouns Correctly: Consistency and Case

CHAPTER 12: THE SIMPLE SENTENCE

page 70　　　*Recognizing Verbs*

a. prepared, packed
b. was burning
c. must have been
d. might accept
e. smell
f. appeared
g. was
h. can cause
i. will volunteer
j. has been commuting
k. complains, irritates, loses
l. are
m. lost
n. reduces
o. combines

page 71　　　*Recognizing Subjects*

a. Rekha, Sanjiv
b. Tomatoes
c. We
d. I
e. Everything
f. anger
g. Cereal, bananas
h. Banks
i. Something
j. Toddlers
k. Cooking, cleaning
l. mosquitoes
m. squirrel
n. She, Nancy
o. They

Recognizing Prepositional Phrases, Subjects, and Verbs

Subjects are underlined; verbs are in *italics*.

a. (In the back of my mind) *was* a plan (for a surprise party).
b. One (of my cousins) *is* a law student (at Dalhousie University).
c. The toy (inside the Cracker Jack box) *was* a big treat (for me).
d. (Over the years), the sisters *grew* closer and *developed* a bond (of intimacy).
e. (Without a doubt), he *deserved* first place (in the writing contest).
f. (From my point) (of view), the job *is* a big promotion (for him).
g. Two (of my nephews) *are spending* the weekend (with me).
h. A house (without a basement) *is* a waste (of money).
i. (During the night), I *must have lost* an earring (between the mattress and the headboard) (of the bed).
j. (At the bakery), we *worked* (around the clock) (on holiday weekends).
k. (Under the circumstances), I *can agree* (with you) (about the traffic ticket).
l. The dog *ran* (into the woods) (at the back) (of the house).
m. John-David *took* a pen (with a very fine point) and *sketched* a figure.
n. A cabin (by the lake) *has been* my dream house (for years).
o. The box (on the counter) *is* the one (with the mail) (in it).

Finding Subjects and Verbs: A Comprehensive Exercise

Subjects are listed first; verbs are in *italics*.

a. lagoon, *is*
b. you, *Have considered*
c. George, *was hoping*
d. mother, *talks*
e. textbooks, stick, *are*
f. You, *might have considered*
g. man, *cut, trimmed*
h. you, *Did try*
i. Dancing, *makes*
j. bowl, *was*
k. She, mother, *designed, sold*
l. One, *runs*
m. reason, *is*
n. Joe, *has called*
o. mother, sister, *will shovel*

CHAPTER 13: THE COMPOUND SENTENCE: COORDINATION

Recognizing Compound Sentences and Adding Commas

a. OK
b. service,
c. role,
d. OK
e. OK
f. tardiness,
g. before,
h. mall,
i. audience,
j. agent,
k. immediately,
l. OK

Writing Compound Sentences 1

Answers may vary.
1. You have to work twice as hard as other people, for you never learned the principles of organization.

2. This seminar is not scheduled for your area, but you might consider attending on-line.
3. You can suffer an energy drain, or you can finally learn how to cope with stress.
4. Communication is the backbone of any effective team, and you need more training in positive communications.
5. Your once secure job goes into a tailspin, so you need new skills to cope, adapt, and stay in control.

page 76   ***Writing Compound Sentences 2***

Answers may vary.
1. You never learned the principles of organization; as a result, you have to work twice as hard as other people.
2. This seminar is not scheduled for your area; however, you might consider attending on-line.
3. You can suffer an energy drain; on the other hand, you can finally learn how to cope with stress.
4. Communication is the backbone of any effective team; therefore, you need more training in positive communications.
5. Your once secure job goes into a tailspin; consequently, you need new skills to cope, adapt, and stay in control.

CHAPTER 14: THE COMPLEX SENTENCE: SUBORDINATION

page 77   ***Punctuating Complex Sentences***

a. movies,
b. OK
c. hockey,
d. OK
e. purchases,

f. OK
g. Alberta,
h. OK
i. community,
j. OK

k. money,
l. OK
m. miles,
n. OK
o. me,

page 78   ***Punctuating Simple, Compound, and Complex Sentences***

a. cup,
b. OK
c. dietician; however,
d. small,
e. major;
f. music,
g. chore; in fact,

h. times;
i. OK
j. job,
k. winter,
l. out; consequently,
m. longer,
n. OK

o. job,
p. forces,
q. manners; moreover,
r. started,
s. us,
t. investment;

CHAPTER 15: AVOIDING RUN-ON SENTENCES AND COMMA SPLICES

page 79   *Correcting Run-On (Fused) Sentences*

a. OK	e. Public Speaking,	h. seven;
b. once;	f. interview,	i. disease,
c. OK	g. morning;	j. birthday,
d. a.m.;		

page 80   *Correcting Comma Splices*

a. town;	e. Friday;	h. OK
b. town;	f. OK	i. Algebra I;
c. OK	g. course;	j. OK
d. Auto;		

page 81   *Coordination: A Comprehensive Exercise*

a. bathroom;	f. little;	k. news,
b. grandfather,	g. teacher; nevertheless,	l. school,
c. day; consequently,	h. license;	m. mathematics; therefore,
d. person,	i. night,	n. school; instead,
e. neighbourhood,	j. adorable; on the other hand,	o. honesty;

CHAPTER 16: AVOIDING SENTENCE FRAGMENTS

page 82   *Checking Groups of Words for Subjects and Verbs*

a. F	d. F	g. F	j. F	m. F
b. F	e. S	h. S	k. F	n. F
c. F	f. S	i. F	l. S	o. F

page 83   *Checking for Dependent-Clause Fragments*

a. F	d. S	g. S	j. F	m. S
b. F	e. F	h. F	k. F	n. F
c. F	f. F	i. F	l. S	o. F

page 84   *Correcting Sentence Fragments*

Answers will vary. Possible answers include
a. Because I couldn't find a place to park, I gave up and drove home.
b. The man in the next booth was arguing with his girlfriend about the price of her meal.
c. With my satellite dish, I can get any television station I want except the local network affiliates.
d. It is hard to concentrate on homework when your neighbours are making noise.
e. I love the music at the Cabana Club, especially the steel band on Wednesday evenings.

f. His purpose is to convince the Planning Council of the need for a playground in the Victoria Hills district.

g. The school children on the field trip were under the supervision of a teacher and a teacher's aide.

h. Since he lost his job last month and couldn't find another, Kevin was unable to make his car payment.

i. Mira wished for a three-day weekend to catch up on her chores and to relax at the lake.

j. While Ruben is an outgoing and talkative person, his brother Edward is extremely shy.

page 86   ***Avoiding Fragments: A Comprehensive Exercise***

a. S	d. F	g. F	j. S	m. F
b. F	e. S	h. F	k. F	n. F
c. F	f. F	i. F	l. S	o. S

CHAPTER 17: USING PARALLELISM IN SENTENCES

page 87   ***Revising Sentences for Parallelism***

Answers will vary. Possibilities include

a. I want a hamburger with onions and Swiss cheese.

b. I have stopped going to that club because the prices are too high, the customers are rude and pushy, and the music is out of style.

c. After we had managed to rake the leaves and bag them, they clew across the yard.

d. OK

e. The recital started at nine; it ended at eleven.

f. The beauty, size, and isolation of the prairie made a lasting impression on me.

g. Art is my most enjoyable, interesting, and challenging class.

h. After the tour of the facilities, the guide gave a brief history of the clinic, showed a short video, and answered any questions.

i. The camp counsellor was eager to get the children settled in, to make them feel comfortable, and to distract them from their homesickness.

j. Seeing the driver run a red light makes me feel angry, indignant, and powerless.

page 89   ***Parallelism: A Comprehensive Exercise***

a.	d. X	g.	j. X
b. X	e. X	h. X	k. X
c. X	f.	i.	l.

CHAPTER 18: CORRECTING PROBLEMS WITH MODIFIERS

page 90   ***Correcting Sentences with Misplaced and Dangling Modifiers***

Answers will vary. Possibilities include

a. When I was stuck in a traffic jam at rush hour, an overheated engine was a real danger.

b. I screamed when I saw the snake slithering across the floor.

c. Last weekend my roommate and I refinished nearly the whole oak table.
d. When he was a tiny baby, his family made the dangerous journey across the continent.
e. After I had survived Biology I, Biology II seemed like an easy course.
f. While exceeding the speed limit, the driver of the tractor trailer ran into a concrete wall.
h. Under a great deal of pressure, we could not possibly meet the deadline.
i. The parents were furious at their son for lingering too long at the party and breaking his curfew.
j. Grabbing a sale item out of the hands of the shopper, the man started a battle.

page 92   *Misplaced and Dangling Modifiers: A Comprehensive Exercise*

a. X	d. X	g. X	j. X	m. X
b. X	e. X	h.	k.	n. X
c.	f.	i.	l.	o. X

CHAPTER 19: USING VERBS CORRECTLY

page 93   *Picking the Correct Verb in the Present Tense*

a. clean	d. memorize	g. distrust	j. brings	m. seem
b. confuse	e. consult	h. cause	k. smiles	n. put
c. smiles	f. search	i. damage	l. causes	o. taste

page 94   *Using the Correct Verb in the Past Tense*

a. signed, raised	d. criticized	g. respected	j. asked
b. called	e. roared, scored	h. pasted	k. wiped, scrubbed
c. approached	f. travelled	i. confirmed	l. suggested

page 95   *Choosing the Correct Form of* **be, have,** *or* **do** *in the Past and Present Tense*

a. does	d. are	g. had	j. had	m. am
b. has	e. does	h. did	k. were	n. do
c. is	f. were	i. were	l. had	o. are

page 96   *Correcting Errors in Verb Forms*

a. The tour guide showed us the great hall of the castle and then <u>led</u> us to the dungeon.
b. The gym teacher meant to be honest about the gymnast's progress, but the teacher <u>shrank</u> from hurting the gymnast's feelings.
c. His brother has brought John nothing but trouble; I don't know how John has <u>borne</u> it for so long.
d. Last night, during the freeze, our pipes burst; it's the first time they have ever <u>broken</u>.
e. While the moviegoers stood in line for tickets, pickpockets <u>crept</u> among the crowd.
f. Three times this week the family has woken in the night because somebody has <u>rung</u> the front doorbell.
g. That company is a reliable one; it has designed and <u>built</u> some of the finest homes in the city.

h. When my boss <u>paid</u> me at the end of the week, I swore I would put that money in a savings account.
i. I feel sorry for Abdul, but he <u>chose</u> to drop out of school, and so he brought her problems on himself.
j. I <u>saw</u> that the other students had finished the exam in only thirty minutes.

page 97   ***Selecting the Correct Verb Form: A Comprehensive Exercise***

a. am	e. realized	i. beaten	m. cost	q. crept
b. smells	f. do	j. blew	n. lay	r. laid
c. goes	g. has	k. bitten	o. lain	s. lain
d. runs	h. is	l. costs	p. fought	t. written

CHAPTER 20: MORE ON VERBS: CONSISTENCY AND VOICE

page 99   ***Correcting Sentences That Are Inconsistent in Tense***

a. On Saturdays I pick up the dry cleaning, <u>shop</u> for groceries, stop at the drug store, and fill the car with gas.
b. Last night a salesman called and <u>offered</u> us a cheaper rate on long distance calls, but the deal sounded fishy.
c. My girlfriend gives me many compliments, and I appreciate them because I know she <u>means</u> what she says.
d. I spent hours selecting a gift and finding the right card; then I <u>planned</u> a special dinner and invited all his friends.
e. I run and work out at a gym every day, so I keep my weight down and <u>release</u> stress
f. Since the restaurant is very popular, people <u>arrive</u> early and line up for a table.
g. My dad was doing all the housework and taking care of the yard while my mom was cooking all the meals and <u>paying</u> the bills.
h. As soon as I get home, I kick off my shoes and <u>flop</u> into a comfortable chair.
i. I love Sundays because I enjoy reading the Sunday papers, I <u>cherish</u> my first, leisurely cup of coffee, and I savour the time to unwind.
j. We visited Niagara-on-the-Lake last fall; we walked down streets full of Victorian homes, <u>shopped</u> in antique stores, and explored the marina.

page 100   ***Distinguishing Between the Past and the Present Perfect Tense***

a. called	d. have been	g. have been	j. was
b. has volunteered	e. prescribed	h. climbed	k. followed
c. learned	f. smoked	i. has been	l. has been

page 101   ***Distinguishing Between the Past and the Past Perfect Tense***

a. had worked	d. studied	g. applauded	j. had simmered
b. had trashed	e. ran	h. had called	k. had taken
c. had given	f. had stolen	i. teased	l. wrote

page 102   ***Rewriting Sentences to Correct Shifts in Voice***

Answers will vary. Possible responses include

a. Yesterday at noon, the club members voted Elaine president.

b. You should choose the cheaper car because it will not break your budget or cost a fortune in car insurance.
c. After the owners met with the bank representatives and discussed their finances last week, they decided to close the restaurant.
d. My neighbour was angry and hurt when he saw that vandals had damaged his garden.
e. If the Crime Stoppers committee can form a plan, Officer Woods will review it.
f. I never understood the dangers of drunk driving until a drunk driver hit a high school classmate; my classmate suffered severe injuries.
g. Hockey fans can be fanatics; they watch every game with intense concentration.
h. The group brainstormed the paper, but each student wrote his or her own draft and submitted it for peer review.
i. The school committee proposed several solutions to the problem of school overcrowding, yet they couldn't agree on one answer.

page 104   ***Consistency and Voice: A Comprehensive Exercise***

a. When Jacob visits his parents, he reminisces about the neighbourhood, <u>fills</u> them in on his latest adventures, and amuses them with funny stories.
b. Tina <u>has</u> danced with the Royal Winnipeg Ballet for several years now.
c. OK
d. OK
e. In a panic about missing the exam, Cody called the teacher's office and pleaded for a make-up test, but the teacher <u>wasn't</u> willing to make an exception for Cody.
f. A few of the volunteers <u>have been</u> paramedics for ten years now.
g. Even if you <u>had</u> worked harder, you couldn't have met that deadline.
h. She <u>had</u> already completed the puzzle when her mother said it was time for bed.
i. Dawn <u>finished</u> her classes at the University of British Columbia last month.
j. Cara bought the invitations, I addressed them, and <u>Charlie mailed them</u>.
k. Whenever I see a movie about lawyers, I wish I <u>had</u> gone to law school.
l. My mother told my brother he should <u>have</u> been more careful with my father's van; repairing the damage to the van would be expensive.
m. The runners were the best in the country because they maintained a strict exercise schedule and <u>adhered</u> to a healthy diet.
n. OK
o. <u>The feuding neighbours finally reached a compromise</u> after they <u>had</u> bickered and complained.
p. I will miss that restaurant because I <u>used</u> to meet my friends there, every Friday after work.
q. The clean-up crew removed dead trees and bushes, bagged the broken bottles and discarded newspapers, and <u>hauled away</u> an old mattress.
r. The locksmith took a bus to work yesterday because he <u>had</u> lost the keys to his car last week.
s. If the police <u>had</u> been five minutes earlier, they could have caught the robbers.
t. He <u>had</u> already replaced the broken glass in the window pane by the time she arrived at the store.

CHAPTER 21: MAKING SUBJECTS AND VERBS AGREE

page 106   ***Making Subjects and Verbs Agree: A Comprehensive Exercise***

a. has	e. Has	i. is	m. was	q. has
b. has	f. is	j. is	n. feels	r. are
c. is	g. is	k. is	o. visit	s. are
d. are	h. has	l. grows	p. are	t. is

CHAPTER 22: USING PRONOUNS CORRECTLY: AGREEMENT AND REFERENCE

page 107   ***Making Pronouns and Antecedents Agree***

a. its   e. his   i. it   m. their   q. they
b. his   f. his or her   j. her   n. they   r. she
c. it   g. her   k. their   o. his   s. its
d. their   h. it   l. her   p it   t. his or her

page 109   ***Rewriting Sentences for Clear Reference of Pronouns***

Answers will vary. Possible rewrites include

a. Pierre warned his father about his father's bad temper.
b. My little brother doesn't mind going to the pediatrician because the staff always give him a cookie.
c. To my surprise, she gave me a gift for my birthday.
d. Because Michelle likes biology, she wants to be a biologist.
e. When I went to pick up my jacket, the clerks told me it hadn't been dry-cleaned yet.
f. Last week my instructor liked my five-page essay.
g. Sunny Airlines provided a great benefits package, including a profit-sharing component, for its employees.
h. When you close up, be sure to put everything back in its place.
i. Raymond's mother is an engineer, so that's why he wants to study engineering.
j. Each of the brothers spent the summer vacation working to pay for tuition at the college of his choice.

CHAPTER 23: USING PRONOUNS CORRECTLY: CONSISTENCY AND CASE

page 111   ***Consistency in Pronouns***

a. Vacations can be a stressful time for me because I try to plan a vacation so special I'll remember it forever.
b. The staff isn't very friendly to us when my husband and I question the cable company about problems with our cable service.
c. My first year working at the store taught me that supervisors will be fair with me if I give them an honest day's work.
d. The children pushed against the fence, eager to see the arrival of the purple dinosaur and the treats he'd give them.
e. Swimmers have to be particularly careful of a riptide; it can carry them out to sea.
f. Ziad and Danica were confused by his speech; he spoke so softly they could hardly hear him.
g. When I arrived late for the movie, the theatre was so crowded I couldn't find a seat anywhere.
h. I never know what treasure I'll discover when I rummage through the merchandise at the thrift shop.
i. People always find comfort in remembering their happy times with loved ones.
j. Drivers have to be careful on mountain roads; if they aren't watching closely, they can drive right off the edge.

CHAPTER 24: PUNCTUATION

a. He asked whether I wanted to go to the movies on Saturday.
b. James questioned Mrs. Mehta about the missing documents.
c. Will he ever stop borrowing money from his sister?
d. I wonder if there will ever be an end to the conflict.
e. Bill loved spicy food; however, it aggravated his stomach problem.
f. OK
g. You were wonderful in the play; you kept the audience amused and entertained.
h. Do you think she is sincere?
i. OK
j. Jessica took good notes in class; she reviewed them carefully before the exam.
k. OK
l. I would never change doctors; I trust Dr. Spinelli.
m. I am not sure whether to go to college near my home.
n. When are you going to make a decision about the wedding?
o. Suzanne can fix the sink; she's a good plumber.

a. Rain or shine, we'll be there for the game on Saturday.
b. I was shocked to see I owed $2,147 on my credit card.
c. OK
d. Artichokes, my husband's favourite vegetable, are easy to cook.
e. Whenever you decide to go, go prepared for any kind of weather.
f. Camera World, which opened last month, is the best place for bargains on film and lenses.
g. I get the freshest fruits and vegetables at the farmers' market, the organic food store, or the neighbourhood produce stand.
h. OK
i. Jane once said, "I'm not a selfish person."
j. You can run from the law, but you can't hide forever.
k. OK
l. Sure, I'll be happy to give Daniel a lift home.
m. August 29, 1996, is the day we got married.
n. When the phone rang, I raced to answer it.
o. Tim became very angry at the rude interruption, yet he managed to control his temper.

Punctuating with Apostrophes

a. Ask Maria if she'll pack David's toys in a couple of sturdy cartons.
b. It's important to return that shirt with its sales receipt if you want your money back.
c. When I saw a sweater left behind at the movies, I didn't pick it up because I wasn't sure it was yours.
d. My grandson was invited to a children's festival at his elementary school.
e. OK
f. Jill asked Jack if he'd take her to Jim and Lisa's party.
g. That century-old house was beautiful; it's a shame its front door couldn't be salvaged.
h. Can't you find some way to discover Phyllis' favourite restaurant?
i. You should see the new movie about extraterrestrials; you'll love the special effects.
j. OK
k. OK
l. My brothers are sure the packages could've been delivered to Mrs. Willis' house instead of to their apartment.
m. Somebody's car keys have fallen behind the dresser; I hope they're not yours.
n. If you get lost in the suburbs, there's an easy way to find your way back to my place.
o. I hope the jacket fits because she's spent hours altering the seams and shoulders.

Punctuating with Colons, Exclamation Marks, Dashes, Parentheses, and Hyphens

a. Every time he goes to the bakery, he brings home a variety of goodies: cinnamon buns, pumpernickel bagels, and jelly doughnuts.
b. The woman who sang opera (the last of the contestants) was the best. OR The woman who sang opera—the last of the contestants—was the best.
c. You're the father of a baby girl!
d. Before I went away to summer camp, my mother told me three things: eat your vegetables, write home, and wear clean underwear.
e. The meeting begins at seven—and you'd better be on time.
f. Fieldbrook Airport (the airport closest to my house) is two hours away. OR Fieldbrook Airport—the airport closest to my house—is two hours away.
g. I see it now; you're an alien invader!
h. The table was beautifully set: china plates shone, glasses sparkled, and coloured napkins glowed.
i. If you're going camping this weekend, take a warm jacket, a hat, and a heavy sleeping bag—the temperature will be freezing.
j. Ellen had some half-baked idea about finishing college in three years.
k. My cousin Elmo (the little snitch) told my mother I'd been stealing the cookies. OR My cousin Elmo—the little snitch—told my mother I'd been stealing the cookies.
l. My father wanted a state-of-the-art computer for his fiftieth birthday.

Punctuating with Quotation Marks, Underlining, and Capital Letters

a. "I'd like to meet him," Eddie said, "but I'm all booked up next week."
b. I have no idea what Dad wants for his birthday.
c. Sammy asked, "Can I borrow your book?"
d. If you want a shortcut to the auditorium, take the Harbourview Expressway to Intercity Mall.
e. Trina complained, "You never clean up the kitchen. You leave the dirty dishes for me to do."
f. He asked if I had ever seen an old movie called *Rocky*, [OR Rocky,] about a fighter.

g. "You need to study more," his teacher said.

h. The only cereal my four-year-old will eat is Kellogg's Raisin Bran.

i. My father loves the song called "The Long and Winding Road."

j. My husband will perform at Riverdale Music Hall in the spring.

k. I chose Margaret Atwood's poem entitled "You Fit Into Me" in a collection called *Power Politics* [OR Power Politics].

page 119   ***Punctuation: A Comprehensive Exercise***

a. Sylvia was sure she had lost the children's winter hats, but she kept looking in the garage and attic.

b. Writing the paper took me hours; consequently, I had no time to study for the quiz in my Introduction to Sociology class.

c. Carmen's Café, which is the best pizza place in town, is expanding its dining area.

d. "If you need a ride to school," she whispered, "you can ride with me."

e. I want to buy an air conditioner because I can't stand hot summer days, humid summer nights, and constant summer hay fever.

f. I wrecked my car and wound up with a bill for $2,042.

g. We used to sing "O Canada" at our meetings.

h. I need to buy some items for our medicine cabinet: aspirin, bandages, cough medicine, and antacid.

i. Lucy can watch the playoffs at my house, or she can watch them on her own television.

j. David left Brampton, Ontario, on April 23, 1981, and settled in Medicine Hat, Alberta.

k. OK

l. Your brother, good or bad, is still a member of your family.

m. I know, Father, that you'd rather be at Thomas' house.

n. When he visited Sarajevo, he saw the way children survive in a war-torn country.

o. Nancy asked, "Are there any volunteers?"

p. Before I attended Middlebrook High School, I had never been to a high school that offered courses like Music Appreciation and French Literature.

q. Susan is taking the summer off; then she'll start college at a school on the East Coast.

r. For ten years, Springfield Chevrolet has been known for its fair deals and low prices; consequently, the company has grown and prospered.

s. Smooth Talk [or *Smooth Talk*], my favourite movie, is based on a short story called "Where Are You Going? Where Have You Been?" by Joyce Carol Oates.

Answer Key

Exercises for Appendix: Grammar for ESL students

page 121   *Identifying and Correcting Present Tense Verbs*

                                            plan

The plot of the movie *Titanic* <u>is</u> a tragic love story. Rose and Cal <u>plans</u> to get married. However,

Rose <u>falls</u> in love with Jack Dawson on the Titanic. He <u>stops</u> her before she <u>jumps</u> over the railing. They
dance   *saves*

<u>dances</u> at the party in steerage. Later she <u>save</u> him by cutting off his handcuffs. Before the ship <u>sinks</u>,
                                         refuses

Rose and Jack <u>help</u> many people to climb to the decks. She <u>refuse</u> to enter the lifeboat with the other rich
            jump

people. The two lovers <u>jumps</u> into the water together; only Jack <u>dies</u> in the cold, cold sea. Despite its sad

ending, the *Titanic* <u>is</u> one of my favourite movies.

page 122   *Revising Verb Tenses 1*

                                is

Another one of my favourite movies ~~will be~~ *Anna and the King*. At the beginning of the film,
travels   *goes*

Anna ~~will travel~~ to Burma to teach the King's children. She ~~is going~~ to teach them English, science, and
                            comes   *fights*

modern ways. Her son Louis ~~will come~~ with her too. First, he ~~will fight~~ with the Crown Prince, and then
         become   *hopes*

they ~~will become~~ close friends. After awhile, Anna ~~is hoping~~ to change the King's ways. During her stay,
    understands   *learns*

she ~~will understand~~ many of the old Siamese traditions; Siam ~~will~~ also ~~learn~~ many things about the British
                                    appreciate

way of life. For their part, the King and his prime minister ~~will appreciate~~ her democratic ideas. However,
  is   *are*

Anna ~~will~~ not ~~be~~ able to help Lady Tuptim or her lover Batel. Overall, there ~~will be~~ many changes in both

Anna's and the King's lives.

page 123   *Revising Verb Tenses 2*

                were   *taught*

Fables ~~are~~ old, old stories. Each fable ~~teaches~~ a lesson or moral. Usually, the characters in the
  were   *acted*   *talked*   *acted*   *were*

fable ~~are~~ animals that ~~act~~ like people. They ~~talk~~ and ~~act~~ silly; they ~~are~~ also clever sometimes.
                                    thought   *ate*

In the fable "The Farmer and the Stork," the farmer ~~thinks~~ *said* that the stork ~~eats~~ *said* his corn. He then

punished
~~punishes~~ not only the stork, but all the other birds as well. The farmer ~~says~~ *said* that all the birds ~~are~~ *were* guilty. The

was   *flocked*   *judged*
moral of the fable ~~is~~ "Birds of a feather ~~flock~~ together." Indeed, people still ~~judge~~ us by our friends and our

were
family, not by who we ~~are~~ as individuals.

page 124   *Revising Contractions*

would not
If people ~~wouldn't~~ be so impatient, driving would be less of an ordeal. If, for instance, the driver

did not   *light has*   *I would*
behind me ~~didn't~~ honk his horn as soon as the ~~light's~~ turned green, both he and ~~I'd~~ probably have lower

would not   *would not*
blood pressure. He ~~wouldn't~~ be irritating himself by pushing so hard. And I ~~wouldn't~~ be reacting by

I am
slowing down, trying to irritate him even more. When I get impatient in traffic, ~~I'm~~ just making a bad

does not
situation worse. My hurry ~~doesn't~~ get me to my destination any faster; it just stresses me out.

does not
The impatient driver ~~doesn't~~ get anywhere; neither does the impatient customer at a restaurant.

does not   *I have*
Impatience at restaurants ~~doesn't~~ pay. ~~I've~~ worked as a hostess at a restaurant, and I know that the

will not
customer who moans and complains about waiting for a table ~~won't~~ get one any faster than the person who

who is
makes the best of the wait. In fact, the customer ~~who's~~ too aggressive or obnoxious is likely to get slower

service from the restaurant staff.

page 125   *Identifying and Correcting Articles*

a
Students face all kinds of problems when they start ~~the~~ college. Some students struggle with lack ▲

a
of basic math skills; others have never learned to write ▲ term paper. Students who were stars in ~~the~~ high

▲
school have to cope with being just another student number at a large post-secondary institution. Students

with ~~the~~ small children have to find a way to be ~~the~~ good parents and ~~the~~ good students too. Although

the   *an*   *The*
many of problems are common, I found ~~a~~ even more typical conflict. ~~Biggest~~ problem in college was
▲   ▲

learning to organize my time.

NOTES

NOTES

NOTES

NOTES

NOTES